Everything Vegetarian

Everything Vegetarian

The Complete Cookbook for a Well-Nourished Life

Wendy Polisi

ROCKRIDGE PRESS

For general information on our other products and services or to obtain technical support, please contact our Customer Care Department within the United States at (866) 744-2665, or outside the United States at (510) 253-0500.

Rockridge Press publishes its books in a variety of electronic and print formats. Some content that appears in print may not be available in electronic books, and vice versa.

Interior and Cover Designer: Brian Lewis
Art Producer: Sue Bischofberger
Editor: Lauren Ladoceour
Production Editor: Matthew Burnett

Photography © Emulsion Studio, pp. ii, vi, 28, 32, 46, 50, 61, 75, 86, 90, 106, 112, 118, 122, 126, 136, 142, 162, 181, 194, 200, 204, and 214; Hélène Dujardin, pp. 25 and 221; Annie Martin, p. 40; Darren Muir, p. 69, 96, 148, 174, and 208; Antonis Achilleos, p. 168; Melina Thompson, p. 186.

Illustration © 2020 Ana Zaja Petrak.

ISBN: Print 978-1-64611-650-8 | eBook 978-1-64611-651-5
R0

Contents

Introduction

Ten years ago, when my exploration of vegetarianism began, no one was more surprised than me. I grew up in a Southern family, where if meat wasn't involved, it wasn't considered a meal. The idea that I would ever eliminate or even reduce my meat consumption was a completely foreign concept.

But in 2010, I found myself standing in a San Diego grocery store, handing a vegetarian magazine to the cashier. I still remember being intrigued by how the simple pasta bowl, garnished with citrus zest and fresh herbs, popped from the bright blue background.

I'm not sure if the impetus was that this East Coast girl picked up the California vibe, but I left the grocery store with the magazine in hand. When I got home, my husband looked at me as if I'd grown a second head and grumbled something under his breath that *perhaps we'd had enough of California living.*

Regardless, I read that magazine until it was tattered and dog-eared, and something inside me stirred. Inspired by the fresh foods and vibrant colors I saw as I turned the pages, I found myself getting inspired in the kitchen in ways that I hadn't in years.

After that, vegetarian recipe after vegetarian recipe was served alongside meat at our family dinners. Time and again, I found myself saying no to meat, fully satisfied with the vegetable dishes on their own.

My creativity in the kitchen increased, and I quickly began coming up with my own creations. I had spent most of my childhood avoiding vegetables, and it surprised me how thrilling I found the challenge of bringing out their best qualities.

As an adventurous kitchen explorer, I found fun ways to keep things exciting, and I hope to inspire you to do the same. A veggie-based life should never be bland and boring. Life is far too short not to be excited by what is on your plate.

In the 150 recipes in this book, I've included enough variations to keep things interesting. Whether you are planning on making a full transition into vegetarianism or merely looking to feed your family more plant-based meals, I hope the time-saving tips, menus, and meal prep suggestions come in handy for you.

Speaking of family: Chances are at least one person in your house eats meat. And that's fine. All of these recipes are designed so that they can be served to omnivores to balance out the meat portion of their meals. After all, part of the joy of cooking is getting to share a meal *together*.

squash

cucumber

leek

to

green beans

scallion

radish

eggplant

bell pepper

parsley

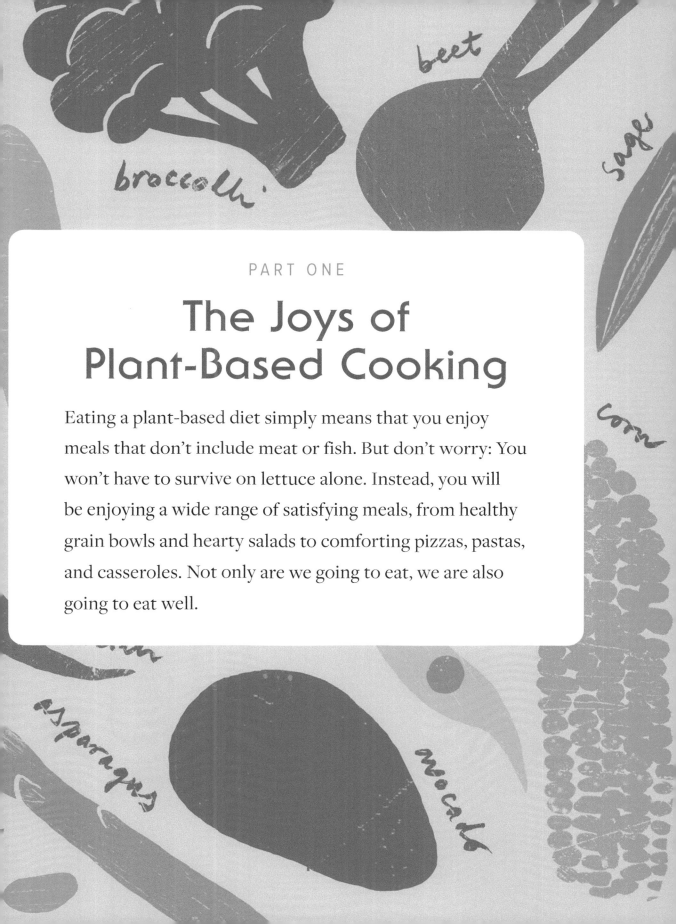

PART ONE

The Joys of Plant-Based Cooking

Eating a plant-based diet simply means that you enjoy meals that don't include meat or fish. But don't worry: You won't have to survive on lettuce alone. Instead, you will be enjoying a wide range of satisfying meals, from healthy grain bowls and hearty salads to comforting pizzas, pastas, and casseroles. Not only are we going to eat, we are also going to eat well.

CHAPTER ONE

Becoming a Vegetarian Cook

So, you've decided to eat more plants? Congratulations, and welcome to the exciting world of vegetarian cooking. Before we dig in to the recipes, let's take a little time for a brief introduction to plant-based cooking, which will guide you and help you create delicious and nourishing meals. We will be taking a look at what it means to be a vegetarian, as well as some of the long-term health benefits of adopting this lifestyle. Explore the tips and tricks, as well as some kitchen essentials you will need, and you'll be on your way.

Are you excited? Let's get this party started.

FALLING IN LOVE WITH THE VEGGIE LIFE

As a child of the 1970s living in the South, I have to admit that the concept of vegetarianism never crossed my mind. Then I went off to college. Within five minutes of our meeting, my roommate informed me she was vegetarian. With only a vague idea of what this meant, I was intrigued. I soon learned that there were many people like her who chose not to eat meat for moral, religious, environmental, or health reasons.

In recent years, more people than ever around the world are transitioning to a vegetarian diet. There is no doubt that eating more plant-based foods is good for both our health and the health of the planet.

Maybe you are here because you are working hard to get healthier and you know that meat-free eating is one way to accomplish this. Or perhaps you have started to question the ethics and sustainability of eating meat. It could be that you have no interest in going vegetarian, but you would like to reduce the amount of meat you eat throughout the week. However you reached this decision, I am here to help you thrive on your journey.

As a girl who gets as excited by a trip to the farmers' market as some do when they stumble on a shoe sale, I can tell you that vegetarian cooking is anything but boring. There is so much room for creativity. As I cook through the seasons, picking the most colorful and vibrant ingredients, it is sometimes hard not to get a little giddy about all the options. Get ready for approachable and deliciously drool-worthy recipes that will leave your taste buds singing.

HOW TO GET STARTED

I want to impress on you that this is a no-pressure zone. Whether you want to serve your family just a few vegetarian meals a week or you are looking to transition to a full-on vegetarian diet, this cookbook is here to be your go-to source of delicious plant-based recipes to cook and share. And it's not just for vegetarians but for anyone who wants to eat meals that burst with flavor, color, and texture. Here are some things to keep in mind when you begin eating more vegetables:

1. **Try new things.** You may never have tried jackfruit and tempeh may look a little strange, but now is the perfect time to branch out. Don't stick to the same plant-based foods you've always eaten. Try new ingredients or cook your old favorites in new ways.

HEALTH BENEFITS WORTH CELEBRATING

There are many benefits to eating vegetarian. But you don't have to give up meat completely to reap some of the benefits of eating more plant-based recipes.

Easier Weight Loss: A study in the *Journal of the American College of Nutrition* found that adults who were eating a reduced-calorie vegetarian diet lost twice as much weight as those who followed an eating routine with the same number of calories that contained meat. Other studies have confirmed that vegetarians tend to have a lower risk of obesity than those who eat meat.

Lower Health Risks: According to a study in *JAMA Internal Medicine*, vegetarians have a 22 percent lower risk of colorectal cancers than carnivores. Additionally, studies indicate that those with a plant-focused diet have a lower risk of high blood pressure and type 2 diabetes. When you say no to processed foods and focus on a whole-foods vegetarian diet, you will eat meals naturally high in antioxidants thanks to all the fruits and vegetables you will be enjoying.

Improved Mood: A study published in *Nutrition Journal* found that people who "eliminate meat, fish, and poultry may cope better with mental stress than omnivores." This would suggest that eating a plant-focused diet supports happiness.

2. **Wash produce.** Even if you buy organic and plan to peel your fruits and veggies, you should always wash them. In addition to pesticides, the surfaces can contain soil and microbes. I recommend a veggie scrub brush for harder vegetables.

3. **Use salt.** If you want flavors to pop, salt is a must. Get in the habit of tasting your food as you cook. Keep in mind that you are getting far less sodium from home-cooked meals than you do processed foods. However, start slow. You can always add more salt, but you can't take it out.

4. **Experiment with herbs.** Fresh or dried, herbs are a great way to wake up the flavors in most foods, and they offer health benefits, too.

5. **Defy meal definitions.** Let go of your ideas about what breakfast, lunch, and dinner should be. You will be surprised at how delicious a salad can be first thing in the morning or how satisfying eggs are for dinner.

6. **Look for bright colors.** Create beautiful plates that boast a rainbow of colors as often as possible, which will ensure that you are getting the widest array of vitamins, minerals, and antioxidants. This means cooking vegetables until they are just tender, being careful to avoid overcooking.

7. **Consider make-ahead meals.** Being prepared is one of the best ways to be successful with any new meal plan, and these time-savers will become your best friend.

8. **Repurpose leftovers.** If you get tired of eating the same thing for more than one meal, consider repurposing them. Today's black beans and turmeric rice can become the base for tomorrow's stir-fry.

9. **Compose a menu.** When you are planning your meals, try to balance out your flavors. Serving a rich and hearty casserole? A simple green salad makes a great side dish. Lighter main dishes go well with heartier sides.

10. **Share with others.** Food is meant to be shared. Don't let that stop now that you have plans to adopt a more veg-centric lifestyle. And when you share your enthusiasm for delicious vegetarian cuisine, you may even inspire your friends and family to eat more plants, too.

YOUR GO-TO INGREDIENTS

Vegetarian cooking can sometimes be labor-intensive, but don't worry. For the recipes in this cookbook, I've tried to keep ingredient lists short and focused primarily on dishes that are fast and easy to make. I've also included a few that are a bit more complex, so you can wow your guests on holidays and other special occasions when spending a little more time in the kitchen isn't a big deal. Here is what you need to make meal preparation enjoyable and stress-free.

CROWD-PLEASING PROTEINS

Beans: A universally loved protein, beans can be used in place of meat in salads, wraps, and casseroles.

Lentils: Lentils are fabulous in hearty soups and a simple way to add protein to salads and grain bowls. They are delicious in veggie burgers, too.

Quinoa: Seasoned well, quinoa makes an excellent substitute for taco meat and is also a great addition to salads and veggie burgers.

Tempeh: The firm texture of tempeh makes it ideal to crumble into chili or tacos in place of ground beef, and it can be used as a substitute for bacon. I also like to cut it into cubes and add it to stir-fry recipes.

Extra-Firm Tofu: Cut it up into very small pieces and toss it into your skillet for a vegan take on an egg scramble, or chop it up and add it to recipes that call for cooked chicken.

COMPLETE PROTEIN, COMPLETELY HEALTHY

Nine essential amino acids must be obtained from food for the body to synthesize protein, absorb nutrients, and repair tissue. While all animal sources of protein provide you with all the essential amino acids that your body needs, there are only a few plant-based foods that do the same thing. Quinoa, amaranth, soy, chia, and hemp all offer complete proteins. Other foods, such as beans, rice, and nuts, do not. This means that eating complementary proteins—that is, two foods that contain what the other one lacks—is necessary to ensure that you are meeting your nutritional needs.

The good news is that it isn't necessary that you eat complementary proteins at each meal, as long as you make sure you are getting them in your diet every day. When you are eating a wide variety of nutritious whole foods, getting all the amino acids you need is relatively simple.

VERSATILE VEGETABLES

Bell Peppers: Available in colors across the rainbow, bell peppers are fabulous in your favorite stir-fry or veggie fajitas, and they make a hearty main course when stuffed with grains and other vegetables.

Cauliflower: The versatile cauliflower works well with other vegetables and readily absorbs flavors from seasonings, whether it's used as a pizza crust, "rice," or "steak."

Onions: The unsung heroes of the vegetable world, onions may not be the main focus of many dishes, but they are one of the best ways I know to make flavors pop. They are great caramelized, braised, and even pickled.

Sweet Potatoes: There are countless ways to enjoy sweet potatoes. I've often enjoyed a simple, satisfying dinner of nothing more than a baked sweet potato and a green salad.

Tomatoes: Though technically a fruit, tomatoes are usually treated as a vegetable. They're great stuffed, cut up into salads, and, of course, cooked into sauces. I am especially fond of slow-roasting them to mimic the umami flavor found in commercially available sun-dried tomatoes.

Winter Squash: Try roasting bite-size cubes of butternut squash for salads and casseroles, or spiralize it for a noodle replacement. Spaghetti squash is a perfect replacement for pasta, and acorn squash really shines when it is roasted or stuffed.

Zucchini: This summer squash is excellent spiralized into "zoodles," and it can even be used grated in baked goods.

GREAT GRAINS

Barley: Both hulled barley and pearl barley are available at most grocery stores. While both have a deliciously chewy texture, I most often choose pearl barley because it cooks faster.

Couscous: You can find this tiny pasta in white, whole-wheat, and even gluten-free forms. All are light, refreshing, and super-quick to prepare.

Farro: Most everyone I know who has tried this buttery grain loves it. Be sure to rinse farro before cooking to keep it from being bitter.

Oats: Everyone knows about using oats in sweet breakfast cereals and baking, but they are equally suited to savory applications.

Quinoa: Technically, quinoa is not a grain but a pseudo-grain—a seed that is treated like a grain. This one comes with protein. Like farro, quinoa should be rinsed before cooking or it can be a bit bitter.

Rice: While white rice can be enjoyed in moderation in a healthy diet, consider experimenting with brown rice or other delicious varieties like black or red rice.

LOW-CARB SUBSTITUTIONS

We all respond to foods differently, and some people may struggle with eating lots of high-carb meals containing pasta, rice, and beans. (This is something I have to watch myself.) Here are some healthy "this for that" swaps to keep your carbs in check:

INSTEAD of mashed potatoes » **TRY** mashed cauliflower

INSTEAD of buns and wraps » **TRY** portobello mushrooms and lettuce leaves

INSTEAD of crackers and chips » **TRY** cheese crisps and kale chips

INSTEAD of sugar » **TRY** monkfruit or Swerve

INSTEAD of all-purpose flour » **TRY** almond or coconut flour

INSTEAD of white rice » **TRY** cauliflower or broccoli rice

INSTEAD of pasta » **TRY** zucchini noodles, butternut squash noodles, or spaghetti squash

INSTEAD of lasagna sheets » **TRY** zucchini or eggplant sliced lengthwise

FAVORITES MADE VEGETARIAN

There are some foods you might assume are vegetarian that actually aren't. Here's what to look for to ensure that what you buy is 100 percent meat-free.

Cheese: Some cheeses, most notably Parmesan, contain animal rennet. Be sure to check labels and look for microbial or plant-based rennet instead.

Wine: Gelatin or fish bladders are commonly used to clarify wine. Unfortunately, this isn't pointed out on a bottle label, but websites like Barnivore.com are good resources for looking up a wine and vintner to see whether they're vegetarian-friendly.

Pesto: It's simple to make pesto either using vegetarian Parmesan or by swapping it for nutritional yeast.

Marshmallows: Marshmallows are made with gelatin, which comes from animal hooves and bones. Look for brands that are labeled "vegan."

Sugar: Many types of sugar are refined using bone char to remove impurities. Seek out brands, such as Imperial Sugar, that do not use animal products.

EXCEPTIONAL FLAVORS

There are so many ways to give dishes rich flavor without using meat. Here are some pantry staples you'll want to make sure to keep on hand.

Oils: For salad dressings and low-heat cooking, I love the rich flavor of extra-virgin olive oil. For higher-heat cooking, I often use regular olive oil or avocado oil.

Vinegar: Balsamic vinegar is one of my go-to choices any time I need a little acid with a hint of sweetness. White wine, red wine, and rice vinegars also come in handy.

Broth: I always keep vegetable broth in the pantry just in case I am short on time and don't have any homemade in the freezer.

Nuts and Seeds: Cashews, pecans, pumpkin seeds, and sunflower seeds are great for a quick snack and also to add a little texture to salads and pasta.

Spices and Seasonings: A small collection of garlic powder, onion powder, chili powder, ground cumin, dried Italian seasoning, dried thyme, and dried basil will give you plenty of options to make flavors pop.

Liquid Smoke: This concentrate imparts the smoky flavors of grilling without the grill. You can find it in the spice aisle at the supermarket.

CHAPTER TWO

Delicious Made Easier

In this section, we'll cover everything you need for vegetarian cooking success. My goal is to help you make everyday cooking a rewarding experience and give you the confidence to share your love of plant-based living.

My list of go-to kitchen essentials can help make transitioning to a veg-centric lifestyle easier. Be sure to review the benefits of meal-prepping and planning and the best way to approach these tasks to streamline your time in the kitchen.

Since most of us have meat-eaters in our lives, I've given simple tips on how to bring a sense of harmony to your kitchen. And for those times when you really want to make things special, take a look at some of my easy ways to build intense flavors and my suggested wine pairings. Finally, I talk about how to read the recipes to ensure kitchen success every time.

KITCHEN TOOLS

If you cook at home at all, chances are you have most everything that you need for easy, satisfying vegetarian cooking. There are a few tools, though, that I think are worth the investment because they can really simplify kitchen tasks.

FOOD PROCESSOR

This handy appliance makes grating cheese and chopping many types of vegetables a cinch. It also makes preparing dips like Cauliflower Hummus (page 24) and Roasted Red Pepper Dip (page 26) quick and easy.

IMMERSION BLENDER

Soups are a snap when you have a handheld immersion blender to puree them. No more working in batches and trying not to burn yourself as you pour hot soup into a countertop blender.

PRESSURE COOKER

Whether you use a stovetop or electric version, this is one gadget you will turn to again and again. It is the ideal way to cook beans and grains in bulk, and it can also make getting an entire meal on the table that much easier.

SLOW COOKER

Thanks to its set-it-and-forget-it benefits, this appliance does all the cooking while you tackle everything else on your to-do list.

SPIRALIZER

You can make veggie noodles with a vegetable peeler, but an inexpensive spiralizer makes the process so much faster. (And if you have kids who resist vegetables, turning them into "noodles" can be a great way to change their minds.)

MAKE-AHEAD HELPERS

Cooking recipe components or staples days ahead of time makes vegetarian cooking simpler and more enjoyable—and keeps the whole family from making unhealthy grab-and-go choices. It can also save you money in terms of eating out less. For example, prepping a big pot of beans and grains on the weekend means that everyone in the family can quickly make veggie bowls or burritos.

WHEN TO PREP

When you prep your meals is entirely based on what works for you and your family. Popular days are Sundays and Wednesdays, but what is most important is finding times that you can follow consistently. Check the tips in the recipes for some handy make-ahead and storage guidelines.

PREP AND COOK

Step 1: Start by reading through each recipe you're going to use. Then get out all the ingredients you'll need. Wash, chop, and measure everything before you begin cooking.

Step 2: Start by cooking any slow cooker recipes or recipes that take a long time, then move on to the rest.

Step 3: Prepare any sauces or dressing you will need to use later.

Step 4: Once you have all the components prepped or cooked, you can put the final dishes together immediately or store each item separately for later assembly.

STORAGE TIPS

1. Let any cooked foods cool before putting them in your refrigerator or freezer. This helps keep your refrigerator and freezer at a constant temperature. (But for food safety issues, don't let anything sit out for more than 1 hour.)

2. It's best to freeze some foods in a single layer on a rimmed baking sheet before transferring them to a storage container. This keeps them from freezing together in a big chunk. I've pointed this out in recipes where necessary.

3. Label whatever you store with the name of the dish and the date that you made it. This is especially important when you are freezing food. Not only will it help you remember what you've got in the freezer, but it will also help you prioritize the order in which you eat the leftovers.

THAWING AND REHEATING

Most made-ahead foods do best when they are thawed overnight in the refrigerator, but in a pinch, you can defrost them in the microwave. I prefer reheating on a stovetop for pasta, rice, or stir-fries. Make sure you add a touch of oil or water to the pan to prevent sticking and drying out.

The oven is the perfect way to reheat dishes like casseroles. Take care to never put a cold glass dish into a warm oven, as this can cause it to crack. Bring a cold dish to room temperature first, or place it in the oven right when you start preheating so it warms slowly.

WHAT NOT TO MAKE AHEAD

Most of the recipes in this book keep and reheat well, but not everything does. A sliced avocado will quickly turn brown, and a dressed salad will become limp after just a few hours. Raw vegetables such as celery, cabbage, and greens do not freeze well, nor does pasta that has not been tossed with a sauce (it's likely to get freezer burn). If you are planning to freeze an uncooked casserole, wait to add any kind of cheese topping until just before you plan on baking it because freezing cheese causes ice crystals to develop and disrupts its structure, making it crumbly and unlikely to melt.

COOKING FOR EVERYONE

From everyday meals for the family to dinner parties, holidays, and celebrations, making food for others is one of the greatest joys of cooking. To make the experience less stressful, try to plan it out as far ahead as possible, taking into account any food intolerances and personal tastes of guests. With the recipes in this book, you will have the confidence to put together satisfying meals that will be loved by vegetarians and omnivores alike.

Try to stick to menus where most of the prep work can be done in advance so you can enjoy the best part of cooking for a crowd: sharing exciting vegetarian food with friends and family. In this way, even the simplest dishes are special because you have prepared them with love.

DINNER GUEST ETIQUETTE

Whether you're a carnivore hosting someone who is vegetarian or vice versa, navigating dinner parties can be tricky. It is important to remember that food is an emotionally charged subject. As a vegetarian, you know what that means, but don't assume that your carnivore friend has even stopped to think that an otherwise vegetarian casserole that uses chicken broth isn't suitable for a vegetarian. (Or that the conventional marshmallows on top of their favorite sweet potato casserole contain animal gelatin.)

If you're a guest, one of the easiest solutions I've found is to explain to the host ahead of time that you have adopted a plant-based lifestyle and offer to bring a dish that works with their menu and that everyone can enjoy. Most people are more than happy to support your choices, and you can do the same when it's your turn to play host.

CREATIVE MENUS

This book has you covered with dishes that will work for households that have a mix of vegetarians and omnivores. Different eating styles should never mean sacrificing the togetherness of family dinners. I frequently create veg-centric meals that work well with simple add-ons for the carnivores in my family. Here are a couple of examples of how you can pair recipes from the book to make interesting meals that all will love. (You will find even more menu ideas in the back of the book on page 224.)

EASY WEEKNIGHT MEAL

Bulgur Taco Salad (page 121)

Mango-Avocado Salsa (page 27)

HOLIDAY MENU

Creamy Pumpkin Soup (page 68)

Radicchio and Kale Salad (page 41)

Cranberry-Apple Wild Rice Pilaf (page 123)

Mushroom Wellington (page 215)

SPECIAL TOUCHES

All of the recipes in this book are delicious as-is, but sometimes you just want a little extra crunch, brightness, or depth. Here are some simple staples to have on hand to elevate your meals.

Caramelized onions add umami and texture to sandwiches, pilafs, and casseroles. Just heat 2 tablespoons unsalted butter in a large skillet over medium-high heat. Add sliced onions to the skillet and stir until the onions become soft and translucent. Lower the heat to medium-low and cook, stirring occasionally, for 15 to 20 minutes, until nicely browned. Store the onions in an airtight container in the refrigerator for up to 1 week.

Slow-roasted tomatoes create a sweeter and more intense tomato flavor that is delicious in salads, sandwiches, and pizzas year-round. Preheat the oven to 325°F and line a rimmed baking sheet with parchment paper. Cut 2 pounds Roma tomatoes in half and put them in a large bowl. Drizzle with enough olive oil to coat and season with salt, pepper, and Italian seasoning. Place the tomatoes cut-side up on the baking sheet and roast for 2 hours 15 minutes to 3 hours, until they shrink to half their original size. Store them in an airtight container in the refrigerator for up to 1 week.

Roasting garlic transforms its sharpness to a spreadable nutty sweetness. Try spreading it on bread, adding it to sauces and pasta, and enjoying it as a topping on pizza. Preheat the oven to 425°F. Slice the top ½ inch or so off an entire head of garlic, enough to expose the cloves. Place the head in a baking dish and drizzle with enough avocado oil to cover. Cover the baking dish with aluminum foil and bake for 45 minutes. Remove the foil and bake for another 15 minutes, or until the garlic is golden brown. Let cool, then squeeze the cloves from the skins. Store the roasted garlic in an airtight container in the refrigerator for up to 1 week or in the freezer for up to 2 months.

HARMONIZING WINES

Many people think that white wine is the go-to choice for all vegetables, but with their different flavor profiles, veggies can go with all sorts of varietals. Here are some excellent pairings that can enhance your meals.

Sauvignon Blanc (herbaceous): Mediterranean Baked Feta (page 29), roasted asparagus, light cream sauces

Chardonnay (oaky or buttery): toasted nuts, roasted squash, Pecan Pesto Pasta (page 189)

Riesling (sweet): candied walnuts, roasted pear salad, Thai-Inspired Salad (page 44)

Pinot Noir (dry and fruit-forward): Mushroom Bolognese (page 163), baked Brie and strawberries, Mushroom Wellington (page 215)

Burgundy (earthy): sautéed mushrooms, roasted eggplant, tomato salad

Syrah (peppery): roasted beets, BBQ jackfruit, heavy red sauces with oregano

Merlot (soft berry): caramelized onions, oven-roasted tomatoes, dark chocolate

Cabernet Sauvignon (big and bold): roasted broccoli, Loaded Mac and Cheese (page 158), Lasagna for All (page 169)

HOW TO READ THE RECIPES

Although all the recipes in this book are straightforward and simple enough for a casual cook to follow, make sure to read them from start to finish before you begin. I've included a few extra features to help you decide what's going to work best for the people who have the pleasure of tasting the fruits of your labor.

Dairy-Free   Gluten-Free   Nut-Free

For example, you'll find allergy labels near the top of each recipe, noting which dishes are dairy-free, gluten-free, and nut-free. You'll see, too, that many of the dishes can easily be made gluten-free by using gluten-free bread, wraps, or pasta. Additional swaps, such as using tamari in place of soy sauce, can also be used to modify many of the recipes.

I've also included some helpful tips at the end of each recipe, with make-ahead instructions and simple substitutions for ingredients that may be hard to find, out of season, or expensive.

Perhaps my number-one tip is to create your mise en place—gathering and prepping all ingredients—before you begin to cook any recipe. That way you can then relax while following the rest of the directions and cook with focus and your whole heart.

squash

cucumber

leek

to

green beans

scallion

radish

eggplant

parsley

bell pepper

PART TWO

Crave-Worthy Recipes

The recipes in this book are approachable, easy to prepare, and flavor-packed. They're also aimed at sparking your creativity and helping you bring out each ingredient's best qualities with flair. You'll find everything you need to cook for whatever the occasion and whoever is at the table.

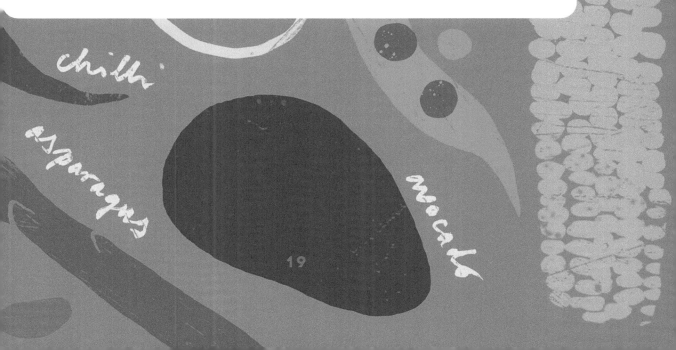

CHAPTER THREE

Snacks and Apps

Vegetarian Bacon

Serves 6 / Prep time: 5 minutes / Cook time: 14 minutes

While nothing perfectly mimics the taste and texture of bacon, don't let that stop you from falling in love with these crispy, smoky morsels. Not only are they fabulous as a snack, but they are also great for VLT Sandwiches (page 91) or in a Vegetarian Cobb Salad (page 49).

1¼ cups large unsweetened coconut flakes

1 tablespoon avocado oil

2 teaspoons soy sauce

1½ teaspoons liquid smoke

1 teaspoon smoked paprika

Salt and black pepper

1. Preheat the oven to 325°F. Line a rimmed baking sheet with parchment paper.

2. In a large bowl, combine the coconut, avocado oil, soy sauce, liquid smoke, and smoked paprika. Season with salt and pepper and toss to coat. Spread out in a single layer on the prepared baking sheet.

3. Bake for 6 minutes. Toss, then bake for another 6 to 8 minutes, until the "bacon" is golden brown. (Make sure you watch very closely in the last few minutes to prevent burning.)

MAKE AHEAD: Store the coconut bacon in an airtight container at room temperature for up to 1 week.

Per serving: Calories: 132; Total fat: 13g; Carbohydrates: 4g; Fiber: 3g; Protein: 1g; Sodium: 104mg

Curried Cashews

Serves 8 / Prep time: 5 minutes / Cook time: 27 minutes

Crunchy nuts never fail to delight. The sweetness of honey perfectly balances the bright and savory curry. These little nibbles are positively addictive.

3 cups raw cashews

¼ cup honey

2 tablespoons unsalted butter

1½ tablespoons curry powder

1 teaspoon ground turmeric

½ teaspoon ground cumin

¼ teaspoon cayenne pepper

2 teaspoons salt

¼ teaspoon black pepper

1. Preheat the oven to 325°F. Line a rimmed baking sheet with parchment paper.

2. Put the cashews in a large bowl.

3. In a small saucepan, combine the honey and butter and cook over medium heat, stirring, until the butter melts and the mixture is smooth. Add the curry powder, turmeric, cumin, cayenne pepper, salt, and black pepper.

4. Pour the mixture over the cashews and stir until well combined. Spread the coated cashews in a single layer on the prepared baking sheet.

5. Bake for 15 minutes. Toss the cashews and bake for another 10 minutes, until golden brown. Let the nuts cool completely on the baking sheet.

MAKE AHEAD: Store these cashews in an airtight container at room temperature for up to 1 week.

Per serving: Calories: 333; Total fat: 25g; Carbohydrates: 25g; Fiber: 2g; Protein: 9g; Sodium: 597mg

Cauliflower Hummus

Serves 6 / Prep time: 10 minutes / Cook time: 20 minutes

No one's ever called me a traditional cook, but this veggie-based hummus surprised me. Cauliflower does a beautiful job standing in for chickpeas, creating a dip for carrots, red bell peppers, cucumber, snap peas, or whatever your version of crudités may be.

1 head cauliflower, cut into florets

1 tablespoon avocado oil

Salt and black pepper

⅔ cup tahini

⅓ cup freshly squeezed lemon juice

1 teaspoon minced garlic

1 teaspoon ground cumin

1 teaspoon everything bagel seasoning, za'atar, or sesame seeds

1. Preheat the oven to 400°F. Line a rimmed baking sheet with parchment paper.

2. Put the cauliflower on the prepared baking sheet, drizzle it with the avocado oil, and toss to coat. Season with salt and pepper. Spread out the cauliflower in a single layer.

3. Roast the cauliflower for 20 minutes, or until tender.

4. Transfer the cauliflower to a food processor, add the tahini, lemon juice, garlic, and cumin, and process until smooth, about 2 minutes. If you prefer a thinner dip, add more lemon juice (or water), 1 tablespoon at a time, until the desired consistency is reached.

5. Sprinkle with your choice of seasoning.

MAKE AHEAD: Store this hummus in an airtight container in the refrigerator for up to 5 days.

Per serving: Calories: 210; Total fat: 17g; Carbohydrates: 12g; Fiber: 5g; Protein: 7g; Sodium: 114mg

Roasted Red Pepper Dip

Serves 6 / Prep time: 10 minutes

I love appetizers that practically make themselves, and this one comes together in a flash—especially if you opt for garlic powder or use jarred minced garlic. We like big flavors in our family, so keep that in mind and feel free to adjust the amount of garlic and red pepper flakes to suit your tastes.

1 (16-ounce) jar roasted red peppers, drained

½ cup slivered almonds

1 tablespoon balsamic vinegar

2 teaspoons minced garlic or ½ teaspoon garlic powder

2 teaspoons dried basil

1 teaspoon red pepper flakes

Salt and black pepper

1. In a blender or food processor, combine the roasted red peppers, almonds, balsamic vinegar, garlic, basil, and red pepper flakes.

2. Process until smooth.

3. Season to taste with salt and pepper and stir to combine.

MAKE AHEAD: Store this dip in an airtight container in the refrigerator for up to 5 days. I prefer to bring it to room temperature prior to serving.

Per serving: Calories: 70; Total fat: 5g; Carbohydrates: 6g; Fiber: 2g; Protein: 3g; Sodium: 3mg

Mango-Avocado Salsa

Serves 6 / Prep time: 15 minutes

Everyone loves Taco Tuesday as a way to shake up the work or school week. This tart, creamy salsa ups the fun while still being super-quick to whip up in time for dinner.

1 (15-ounce) can black beans, drained and rinsed

½ red bell pepper, seeded and diced

½ medium red onion, diced

1 poblano pepper, diced

1 cup diced mango

⅓ cup chopped fresh cilantro

3 tablespoons rice vinegar

1 tablespoon freshly squeezed orange juice

1 tablespoon extra-virgin olive oil

Salt and black pepper

½ avocado, pitted, peeled, and diced

1. In a medium bowl, combine the black beans, bell pepper, red onion, poblano pepper, mango, and cilantro.

2. In a small bowl, whisk together the rice vinegar, orange juice, and olive oil. Drizzle the dressing over the black bean mixture and stir to combine. Season the salsa to taste with salt and pepper.

3. Just before serving, toss in the avocado.

MAKE AHEAD: Except for the avocado, this salsa can be made up to 3 days ahead of time and stored in an airtight container in the refrigerator. To prevent browning, dice the avocado and add it just before serving.

Per serving: Calories: 126; Total fat: 4g; Carbohydrates: 18g; Fiber: 6g; Protein: 4g; Sodium: 3mg

Mediterranean Baked Feta

Serves 6 / Prep time: 10 minutes / Cook time: 20 minutes

The briny punch of feta in this showstopper recipe plays with the vegetables, seasonings, and balsamic vinegar to create a party in your mouth. Serve with pita chips.

1 (8-ounce) block feta cheese, drained

¼ cup diced red onion

½ cup halved cherry tomatoes

⅓ cup sliced pitted kalamata olives

½ teaspoon dried oregano

Black pepper

1 tablespoon olive oil

1½ teaspoons balsamic vinegar

1. Preheat the oven to 400°F.

2. Place the feta in the center of a small baking dish. Top with the red onion, tomatoes, and olives. Sprinkle with the oregano and season with black pepper. Drizzle with the olive oil and balsamic vinegar.

3. Bake for 20 minutes. Serve warm.

MAKE AHEAD: This recipe can be assembled and stored in an airtight container in the refrigerator for up to 2 days, then baked as directed. Leftovers (if you have any!) will keep in an airtight container in the refrigerator for up to 4 days.

Per serving: Calories: 160; Total fat: 12g; Carbohydrates: 11g; Fiber: 1g; Protein: <1g; Sodium: 506mg

Buffalo Cauliflower Bites

Serves 6 / Prep time: 15 minutes / Cook time: 25 minutes

When I first created this recipe, I ended up making it three days in a row at my family's request. You are going to love the buttery, tangy sauce paired with surprisingly crispy cauliflower.

3 large eggs

¾ cup all-purpose flour

½ cup finely grated vegetarian Parmesan cheese

1 teaspoon garlic powder

½ teaspoon smoked paprika

Salt and black pepper

1 large head cauliflower, cut into large florets

1 cup buffalo sauce

2 tablespoons unsalted butter

1. Preheat the oven to 400°F. Line a rimmed baking sheet with parchment paper and coat it with cooking spray.

2. In a shallow bowl, beat the eggs.

3. In a separate bowl, combine the flour, Parmesan, garlic powder, and smoked paprika and season the mixture with salt and pepper.

4. Dip the cauliflower florets into the eggs, dredge them in the flour mixture, and place them on the prepared baking sheet. If necessary, use a second baking sheet to avoid overcrowding.

5. Roast for 15 minutes, then flip the cauliflower florets and spray them with cooking spray. Continue roasting for another 5 to 10 minutes, until browned and crispy.

6. When the cauliflower is nearly done, warm the buffalo sauce and butter in a small saucepan over medium-low heat. Toss the cauliflower with the sauce.

MAKE AHEAD: This dish is best served right away, but if necessary, it can be made up to 1 day ahead and stored in an airtight container in the refrigerator.

Per serving: Calories: 189; Total fat: 8g; Carbohydrates: 22g; Fiber: 3g; Protein: 8g; Sodium: 1427mg

Spicy Patatas Bravas

Serves 6 / Prep time: 15 minutes / Cook time: 25 minutes

Fried potatoes are delicious on their own, but when you add a spicy dipping sauce, your taste buds are guaranteed to do a happy dance.

2 pounds russet potatoes, peeled and cut into ½-inch pieces

2 tablespoons white vinegar

3 tablespoons avocado oil

Salt

2 tablespoons mayonnaise

2 tablespoons plain yogurt

1 tablespoon soy sauce

1 tablespoon ketchup

1 teaspoon minced garlic

1 teaspoon smoked paprika

¼ teaspoon cayenne pepper

1. Line a rimmed baking sheet with paper towels.

2. Put the potatoes in a large pot and cover them with water by 1½ inches. Add the vinegar and bring to a boil over high heat. Lower the heat to medium and simmer for 5 minutes. Drain, then transfer the potatoes to the prepared baking sheet.

3. In a large skillet, warm the oil over medium-high heat. Add half of the potatoes and cook, turning occasionally, until crisp and brown, 10 to 15 minutes. Using a slotted spoon, transfer the potatoes to the same baking sheet lined with fresh paper towels. Season them with salt. Repeat with the remaining potatoes.

4. In a small bowl, stir together the mayonnaise, yogurt, soy sauce, ketchup, minced garlic, smoked paprika, and cayenne. Serve the potatoes warm with the spicy dipping sauce on the side.

MAKE AHEAD: Store the sauce in an airtight container in the refrigerator for up to 3 days.

Per serving: Calories: 220; Total fat: 11g; Carbohydrates: 29g; Fiber: 2g; Protein: 4g; Sodium: 208mg

Southwestern Egg Rolls

Serves 6 / Prep time: 10 minutes / Cook time: 20 minutes

Here's a surprisingly easy vegetarian version of a take-out favorite. I bake these egg rolls, but you can also fry them until golden brown. Serve them alone or with a tangy dipping sauce.

1 (15-ounce) can black beans, drained and rinsed

1 jalapeño, seeded and diced

1 red bell pepper, seeded and diced

1 cup frozen corn, thawed

1 cup shredded cheddar cheese

1 tablespoon chili powder

1 teaspoon ground cumin

Salt and black pepper

12 egg roll wrappers

1. Preheat the oven to 400°F. Line a rimmed baking sheet with parchment paper and coat it well with cooking spray.

2. In a large bowl, toss together the black beans, jalapeño, bell pepper, corn, cheddar cheese, chili powder, and cumin, then season the mixture with salt and pepper.

3. Coat the egg roll wrappers with cooking spray. Divide the filling equally among the wrappers and roll them according to the package instructions. Place the egg rolls seam-side down on the prepared baking sheet and coat the tops with cooking spray.

4. Bake for 15 to 20 minutes, until golden brown. Serve warm.

MAKE AHEAD: These egg rolls can be assembled, wrapped in plastic wrap, and frozen for up to 2 months. Follow the recipe instructions when ready to bake.

Per serving: Calories: 288; Total fat: 7g; Carbohydrates: 45g; Fiber: 6g; Protein: 13g; Sodium: 432mg

Sun-Dried Tomato and Cream Cheese Stuffed Mushrooms

Serves 6 / Prep time: 15 minutes / Cook time: 17 minutes

These are quick to make and even quicker to disappear! They are a nice choice for entertaining, since all the prep work can be done in advance.

12 ounces small mushroom caps

1 tablespoon olive oil

1 cup chopped red onion

⅓ cup minced sun-dried tomatoes

1 tablespoon minced garlic

Salt and black pepper

4 ounces cream cheese, softened

¼ cup grated vegetarian Parmesan cheese

1. Preheat the oven to 400°F. Line a rimmed baking sheet with parchment paper.

2. Place the mushroom caps, stem-side down, on the prepared baking sheet. Bake for 6 minutes. Transfer the mushrooms to a double layer of paper towels. Turn the oven to broil.

3. In a small skillet, heat the oil over medium heat. Add the onion and sauté for 6 minutes. Add the sun-dried tomatoes and sauté for 2 minutes. Add the garlic and sauté for 30 seconds. Season with salt and pepper.

4. Transfer the mixture to a food processor, add the cream cheese, and pulse until combined.

5. Spoon the mixture into the mushroom caps and place them, filled-side up, on the same baking sheet. Sprinkle the mushrooms with the Parmesan.

6. Broil for 3 to 5 minutes, until the cheese is melted and lightly browned.

MAKE AHEAD: The mushrooms can be stuffed up to 2 days ahead of time and stored in an airtight container in the refrigerator, then baked.

Per serving: Calories: 135; Total fat: 10g; Carbohydrates: 9g; Fiber: 1g; Protein: 4g; Sodium: 132mg

CHAPTER FOUR

Salads

Black Bean Tortilla Salad with Pickled Onion

Serves 4 / Prep time: 15 minutes / Cook time: 10 minutes

Crispy tortilla strips offer pops of texture in this salad that I think you will find madly addictive. Serve this as a main course or alongside any meal with Southwestern flavors.

4 corn tortillas, cut in half and then into strips

Salt and black pepper

1 small red onion, sliced

1 cup water

1 cup red wine vinegar, divided

¾ cup extra-virgin olive oil

1 teaspoon smoked paprika

1 head romaine lettuce, chopped

1 (15-ounce) can black beans, drained and rinsed

1 cup frozen corn, thawed

1 cup cherry tomatoes, halved

1 avocado, pitted, peeled, and sliced

1. Preheat the oven to 350°F. Line a rimmed baking sheet with parchment paper.

2. Spread out the tortilla strips on the prepared baking sheet and coat them with cooking spray. Season the strips with salt and pepper. Bake for 10 minutes, turning halfway through.

3. Meanwhile, put the sliced onions in a small bowl. In a small saucepan, bring the water and ¾ cup vinegar to a boil over medium-high heat. Pour the mixture over the onions.

4. In a small bowl, combine the olive oil, remaining ¼ cup vinegar, and smoked paprika. Season with salt and pepper.

5. When the tortilla strips are done, drain the onions. In a large bowl, combine the romaine lettuce, black beans, corn, and cherry tomatoes. Add the dressing and toss to coat. Top with the pickled onion, avocado, and tortilla strips.

MAKE AHEAD: Store the toasted tortilla strips in an airtight container at room temperature for up to 4 days.

Per serving: Calories: 660; Total fat: 48g; Carbohydrates: 50g; Fiber: 17g; Protein: 12g; Sodium: 35mg

Spiralized Zucchini Salad with Tomatoes and Goat Cheese

Serves 4 / Prep time: 20 minutes

If you are a zucchini lover like me, you are going to go wild for this spiralized salad. It is one I turn to again and again during the summer, when zucchini is in abundant supply.

2 medium zucchini, spiralized

1 cup halved grape tomatoes

¼ cup extra-virgin olive oil

2 tablespoons red wine vinegar

Salt and black pepper

¼ teaspoon red pepper flakes

1½ ounces goat cheese, crumbled

¼ cup thinly sliced fresh basil

1 tablespoon sunflower seeds

1. In a medium bowl, toss the zucchini noodles with the tomatoes. Add the oil and vinegar and season with salt, pepper, and the red pepper flakes. Toss until well combined.

2. Top with the goat cheese, basil, and sunflower seeds.

MAKE AHEAD: Store the zucchini noodles in an airtight container in the refrigerator for up to 5 days.

Per serving: Calories: 197; Total fat: 18g; Carbohydrates: 5g; Fiber: 2g; Protein: 5g; Sodium: 56mg

Radicchio and Kale Salad

Serves 4 / Prep time: 15 minutes

This simple salad makes for an easy weeknight meal, but it's also pretty enough for your holiday table. Balsamic vinegar can vary wildly in flavor, so make sure you taste the dressing before adding sweetener.

½ cup plus 1 tablespoon extra-virgin olive oil, divided

3 tablespoons balsamic vinegar

1 tablespoon Dijon mustard

1 teaspoon minced garlic

Salt and black pepper

1 to 2 tablespoons sweetener of choice (optional)

1 bunch kale, stemmed and chopped

1 head radicchio, roughly chopped

⅓ cup toasted pine nuts

⅓ cup pomegranate arils

1. In a blender, combine ½ cup olive oil, the balsamic vinegar, Dijon mustard, and garlic, season the mixture with salt and pepper, and process until smooth. Taste and add sweetener (if using).

2. Put the kale in a large bowl and massage the leaves with the remaining 1 tablespoon oil for 2 minutes. Add the radicchio, pine nuts, and pomegranate arils and toss. Add the desired amount of dressing and toss to coat.

MAKE AHEAD: Store the undressed salad in an airtight container in the refrigerator for up to 2 days. Add the dressing just before serving.

Per serving: Calories: 382; Total fat: 39g; Carbohydrates: 8g; Fiber: 2g; Protein: 3g; Sodium: 105mg

Poppy Seed, Grape, and Tempeh Salad

Serves 4 / Prep time: 15 minutes / Cook time: 10 minutes

This tempeh salad is a tasty make-ahead lunch to assemble during your weekend meal prep. I like it served over a bed of butter lettuce, but you can also roll it up in a wrap.

1 (1-pound) package tempeh

3 celery stalks, diced

2 cups halved red grapes

½ cup diced red onion

⅓ cup chopped cashews

¼ cup mayonnaise

3 tablespoons freshly squeezed orange juice

1 tablespoon apple cider vinegar

1 tablespoon Dijon mustard

1 tablespoon poppy seeds

Salt and black pepper

1. Place a steamer basket in a large pot, pour in 2 inches of water, and bring it to a boil over high heat. Lower the heat to medium, add the tempeh, cover, and steam for 10 minutes. Cut the tempeh into bite-size pieces.

2. In a large bowl, combine the tempeh, celery, grapes, red onion, and cashews.

3. In a small bowl, whisk together the mayonnaise, orange juice, apple cider vinegar, Dijon mustard, and poppy seeds, then season with salt and pepper.

4. Pour the dressing over the tempeh mixture and toss to combine. Cover and refrigerate for at least 1 hour. Toss again just before serving.

MAKE AHEAD: Store this salad in an airtight container in the refrigerator for up to 5 days.

Per serving: Calories: 497; Total fat: 27g; Carbohydrates: 37g; Fiber: 16g; Protein: 29g; Sodium: 206mg

Broccoli Slaw Salad

Serves 6 / Prep time: 10 minutes

This is one of my favorite sides to serve for summer entertaining, though it works well year-round. Crunchy broccoli and almonds, sweet cranberries, and a touch of punchy red onion are tossed in a sweet dressing for the perfect combination of flavors.

1 (16-ounce) bag broccoli slaw

1 (6-ounce) bag broccoli florets

½ cup diced red onion

½ cup sliced almonds

⅓ cup dried cranberries

¼ cup mayonnaise

2 tablespoons freshly squeezed lemon juice

2 tablespoons sweetener of choice

½ teaspoon celery seed

Salt and black pepper

1. In a large bowl, toss together the broccoli slaw, broccoli florets, red onion, almonds, and cranberries.

2. In a small bowl, whisk together the mayonnaise, lemon juice, sweetener, and celery seed. Season with salt and pepper.

3. Toss the dressing with the broccoli mixture and serve immediately.

MAKE AHEAD: Store the dressing in an airtight container in the refrigerator for up to 5 days. Store the salad in an airtight container in the refrigerator for up to 2 days. Add the dressing just before serving.

Per serving (with honey as the sweetener): Calories: 210; Total fat: 12g; Carbohydrates: 23g; Fiber: 5g; Protein: 5g; Sodium: 89mg

Thai-Inspired Salad

Serves 6 / Prep time: 15 minutes

This crunchy salad has a peanut dressing that is out of this world. I often double the recipe and use it as a dipping sauce for raw or steamed veggies.

½ cup peanut butter

⅓ cup hot water

¼ cup freshly squeezed lime juice

2 tablespoons soy sauce

1 tablespoon minced fresh ginger

1 teaspoon minced garlic

Salt and black pepper

4 cups shredded cabbage

3 carrots, grated

2 scallions, chopped

½ cup fresh basil or cilantro leaves

⅓ cup peanuts

1. In a small bowl, whisk together the peanut butter, water, lime juice, soy sauce, ginger, and garlic. Season the dressing with salt and pepper.

2. In a large bowl, combine the cabbage, carrots, and scallions. Toss with the desired amount of dressing and top with the fresh basil and peanuts.

MAKE AHEAD: Store the dressing in an airtight container in the refrigerator for up to 5 days. You can make the salad through the scallions and store it in an airtight container in the refrigerator for up to 2 days, then add the dressing, basil, and peanuts when you're ready to serve.

Per serving: Calories: 207; Total fat: 15g; Carbohydrates: 14g; Fiber: 4g; Protein: 8g; Sodium: 328mg

Brussels Sprout Salad with Avocado

Serves 6 / Prep time: 20 minutes / Cook time: 7 minutes

You won't believe how good this salad is! Sturdy kale and Brussels sprouts hold up for a few days in the refrigerator, even when dressed, making this recipe perfect for meal prep.

1 tablespoon avocado oil

1 pound Brussels sprouts, trimmed and shredded

4 cups finely chopped kale

4 ounces feta cheese, crumbled

½ cup extra-virgin olive oil

2 tablespoons freshly squeezed lemon juice

2 tablespoons apple cider vinegar

1 tablespoon Dijon mustard

1 teaspoon minced garlic

Salt and black pepper

1 avocado, pitted, peeled, and chopped

¼ cup chopped toasted pecans

1. In a large skillet, warm the avocado oil over medium heat. Add the Brussels sprouts and sauté until lightly charred, 5 to 7 minutes. Let them cool.

2. In a large bowl, toss together the Brussels sprouts, kale, and feta.

3. In a blender, combine the olive oil, lemon juice, apple cider vinegar, Dijon mustard, and garlic and blend until smooth. Season the dressing with salt and pepper.

4. Toss the salad with the desired amount of dressing, then top it with the avocado and pecans.

MAKE AHEAD: Store this salad, without the avocado, in an airtight container in the refrigerator for up to 2 days. Add the avocado just before serving.

Per serving: Calories: 341; Total fat: 32g; Carbohydrates: 11g; Fiber: 6g; Protein: 7g; Sodium: 304mg

Fried Goat Cheese Salad

Serves 6 / Prep time: 15 minutes / Cook time: 4 minutes

When you want to wow your friends and family, this salad is the perfect solution. Warm, creamy goat cheese balances perfectly with peppery arugula and sweet grapes.

1 cup gluten-free bread crumbs

Salt and black pepper

1 large egg

10 ounces goat cheese, cut into 6 rounds

2 tablespoons avocado oil

½ cup balsamic vinegar

2 tablespoons maple syrup

1 tablespoon Dijon mustard

1 teaspoon minced garlic

½ cup extra-virgin olive oil

5 ounces baby arugula

1 cup halved seedless red grapes

½ red onion, thinly sliced

¼ cup chopped toasted walnuts

1. Line a plate with parchment paper.

2. Put the bread crumbs in a shallow bowl and season them with salt and pepper. In another shallow bowl, beat the egg. Dip each cheese round in the egg, then dredge it in the bread crumbs to coat. Transfer the rounds to the prepared plate.

3. In a large skillet, heat the avocado oil over medium-high heat. Add the goat cheese rounds and cook until browned, 1 to 2 minutes per side. Transfer the rounds to the same plate.

4. In a blender, combine the balsamic vinegar, maple syrup, Dijon mustard, and garlic and blend until smooth. With the motor running, add the olive oil in a steady stream. Season with salt and pepper.

5. In a large bowl, toss the arugula, grapes, onion, and walnuts with the dressing. Transfer to serving plates and top with the goat cheese rounds.

MAKE AHEAD: Store the dressing in an airtight container in the refrigerator for up to 5 days.

Per serving: Calories: 499; Total fat: 37g; Carbohydrates: 27g; Fiber: 2g; Protein: 15g; Sodium: 289mg

Kale and Roasted Beet Salad with Candied Walnuts

Serves 6 / Prep time: 15 minutes / Cook time: 1 hour 30 minutes

With earthy beets, sweet candied walnuts, and a punchy balsamic vinaigrette, this is a great recipe to up your salad game. Alternatively, you can use the dressing for the Fried Goat Cheese Salad (page 47).

6 medium or 3 large beets, trimmed

½ cup halved walnuts

2 tablespoons maple syrup

Salt and black pepper

2 bunches kale, stemmed and thinly sliced

1 tablespoon extra-virgin olive oil

½ cup dried cranberries

⅓ cup balsamic vinegar dressing

1. Preheat the oven to 375°F. Line a plate with parchment paper.

2. Put the beets in a large baking dish and cover it with aluminum foil. Roast for 1½ hours, or until tender. Let the beets cool, then peel and cut them into thin matchsticks.

3. In a skillet, combine the walnuts, maple syrup, and a pinch of salt and cook, stirring, over medium-high heat for 4 minutes. Transfer the nuts to the prepared plate and let them cool.

4. In a large bowl, massage the kale with the olive oil for 2 minutes. Season it with salt and pepper.

5. Add the beets and cranberries and toss the salad with the dressing. Top with the candied walnuts.

MAKE AHEAD: Store this salad in an airtight container in the refrigerator for up to 2 days. Add the dressing just before serving.

Per serving: Calories: 201; Total fat: 10g; Carbohydrates: 28g; Fiber: 5g; Protein: 4g; Sodium: 133mg

Vegetarian Cobb Salad

Serves 6 / Prep time: 15 minutes

The contrast between crunchy romaine, crispy "bacon," creamy blue cheese, and avocado is enough to swoon over. Still, the dressing is the star of the show, bringing everything together with a zippy, refreshing punch.

⅓ cup olive oil

3 tablespoons red wine vinegar

1 tablespoon freshly squeezed lemon juice

1 tablespoon Dijon mustard

1 teaspoon minced garlic

1 teaspoon sugar

½ teaspoon red pepper flakes

Salt and black pepper

1 (15-ounce) can chickpeas

1 avocado

1 head romaine lettuce

1 recipe Vegetarian Bacon (page 22)

3 large hard-boiled eggs, sliced

2 plum tomatoes, diced

⅓ cup crumbled blue cheese

1. In a blender, combine the olive oil, red wine vinegar, lemon juice, Dijon mustard, garlic, sugar, and red pepper flakes and blend until smooth. Season the dressing with salt and pepper.

2. Rinse and drain the chickpeas. Pit, peel, and dice the avocado.

3. In a large bowl, toss together the lettuce, chickpeas, vegetarian bacon, eggs, avocado, tomatoes, and blue cheese.

4. Add the dressing, toss, and serve immediately.

MAKE AHEAD: Store the dressing in an airtight container in the refrigerator for up to 5 days. Store the salad, minus the avocado and vegetarian bacon, in an airtight container in the refrigerator for up to 1 day.

Per serving: Calories: 430; Total fat: 35g; Carbohydrates: 22g; Fiber: 10g; Protein: 11g; Sodium: 386mg

Fall Panzanella

Serves 6 / Prep time: 20 minutes / Cook time: 1 hour 45 minutes

Earthy beets contrast beautifully with tart apple and sweet potatoes, and for a little extra crunch, toasted pecans are an excellent addition.

4 beets, trimmed

2 sweet potatoes, peeled and cut into
½-inch pieces

¾ cup plus 2 tablespoons olive oil, divided

Salt and black pepper

2 cups (½-inch) cubes stale bread

6 cups chopped butter lettuce

1 Granny Smith apple, cored and sliced

¼ cup apple cider vinegar

3 tablespoons honey

1 teaspoon minced garlic

1. Preheat the oven to 375°F. Put the beets in a large baking dish and cover with foil. Roast for 1 hour.

2. Toss the sweet potatoes with 2 tablespoons olive oil on a parchment-lined baking sheet. Season with salt and pepper and spread in a single layer.

3. Place the sweet potatoes in the oven along with the beets and roast for 30 to 45 minutes, tossing the potatoes halfway through, until tender. When the beets are cool enough to handle, peel and chop them.

4. Meanwhile, heat ¼ cup olive oil in a large skillet over medium heat. Add the bread cubes, season them with salt and pepper, and cook, stirring, until the bread is golden, about 7 minutes.

5. In a large bowl, toss the lettuce with the beets, sweet potatoes, bread, and apple.

6. In a blender, blend the vinegar, honey, garlic, and the remaining ½ cup olive oil until smooth. Season with salt and pepper. Toss the salad with the dressing and serve immediately.

MAKE AHEAD: Store the roasted beets and sweet potatoes in an airtight container in the refrigerator for up to 5 days.

Per serving: Calories: 428; Total fat: 32g; Carbohydrates: 34g; Fiber: 5g; Protein: 4g; Sodium: 128mg

Fattoush Salad

Serves 4 / Prep time: 15 minutes

This crunchy, fresh salad is my idea of perfection. The addition of pita bread makes it a satisfying meal. If you don't have sumac, you can substitute grated lemon zest or lemon pepper.

1 small head romaine lettuce, sliced

2 tomatoes, chopped

1 red onion, thinly sliced

1 cucumber, diced

⅓ cup chopped fresh mint and/or parsley

⅓ cup extra-virgin olive oil

3 tablespoons freshly squeezed lemon juice

2 teaspoons ground sumac

1 teaspoon minced garlic

Salt and black pepper

2 pitas, toasted

1. In a large bowl, toss together the lettuce, tomatoes, red onion, cucumber, and herbs.

2. In a blender, combine the olive oil, lemon juice, sumac, and garlic and blend until smooth. Season with salt and pepper.

3. Add the desired amount of dressing to the salad and toss to combine.

4. Tear the pitas into bite-size pieces and add them to the salad.

MAKE AHEAD: Store the toasted pitas in an airtight container at room temperature for up to 5 days. Store the dressing in an airtight container in the refrigerator for up to 5 days.

Per serving: Calories: 303; Total fat: 19g; Carbohydrates: 30g; Fiber: 7g; Protein: 6g; Sodium: 193mg

Chinese-Inspired "Chicken" Salad

Serves 6 / Prep time: 15 minutes / Cook time: 10 minutes

In this Asian-style salad, browned tempeh is perfectly seasoned and combined with crisp cabbage and carrots, sweet mandarin oranges, and crunchy chow mein noodles.

1 (1-pound) package tempeh

¼ cup plus 2 tablespoons soy sauce, divided

3 teaspoons toasted sesame oil, divided

Salt and black pepper

½ cup plus 2 tablespoons olive oil, divided

4 cups chopped cabbage

½ cup shredded carrots

1 (11-ounce) can mandarin oranges, drained with 2 tablespoons juice reserved

¼ cup rice wine vinegar

1 teaspoon minced fresh ginger

½ cup chow mein noodles

1. Place a steamer basket in a large pot, pour in 2 inches of water, and bring it to a boil over high heat. Lower the heat to medium, add the tempeh, cover, and steam for 10 minutes. Cut the tempeh into small pieces.

2. In a small bowl, toss the tempeh with 2 tablespoons soy sauce and 1 teaspoon sesame oil. Season with salt and pepper.

3. In a skillet, warm 2 tablespoons olive oil over medium heat. Sauté the tempeh until browned, 3 to 4 minutes.

4. In a large bowl, toss together the cabbage, carrots, and mandarin oranges.

5. In a blender, combine the remaining ½ cup olive oil, remaining ¼ cup soy sauce, remaining 2 teaspoons sesame oil, the reserved mandarin juice, vinegar, and ginger and blend until smooth. Season the dressing with salt and pepper.

6. Add the dressing to the cabbage mixture and toss to combine. Top the salad with the tempeh and chow mein noodles.

MAKE-AHEAD: Store the browned tempeh in an airtight container in the refrigerator for up to 3 days.

Per serving: Calories: 454; Total fat: 33g; Carbohydrates: 23g; Fiber: 11g; Protein: 20g; Sodium: 928mg

Roasted Vegetable Salad with Green Goddess Dressing

Serves 6 / Prep time: 15 minutes / Cook time: 25 minutes

When my son wanted seconds, I knew this salad was a keeper. I drizzle the dressing over grain bowls or use it as a dipping sauce for Italian Farro Cakes (page 116).

8 ounces carrots, peeled and chopped

8 ounces radishes, halved

8 ounces asparagus, trimmed

1 red onion, cut into wedges

2 tablespoons avocado oil

Salt and black pepper

1 to 3 tablespoons water

1 avocado, pitted, peeled, and diced

⅓ cup plain yogurt

2 tablespoons freshly squeezed lemon juice

½ cup chopped fresh parsley, chives, or basil

1 teaspoon minced garlic

8 cups chopped romaine lettuce

1. Preheat the oven to 425°F. Line a rimmed baking sheet with parchment paper.

2. In a large bowl, toss the carrots, radishes, asparagus, and red onion with the oil. Season the vegetables with salt and pepper.

3. Arrange the vegetables in a single layer on the prepared baking sheet and roast for 20 to 25 minutes, until crisp-tender. Let them cool slightly.

4. In a food processor, combine the avocado, yogurt, lemon juice, herbs, and garlic and process until smooth. Season the dressing with salt and pepper. Add the water, 1 tablespoon at a time, and process until it reaches the desired consistency.

5. In a large bowl, toss the romaine and roasted vegetables with the dressing.

MAKE AHEAD: The dressing can be made up to 2 days ahead; transfer it to a small bowl, cover it with plastic wrap touching the surface to help prevent the avocado from browning, and store it in the refrigerator.

Per serving: Calories: 137; Total fat: 9g; Carbohydrates: 14g; Fiber: 6g; Protein: 4g; Sodium: 58mg

BBQ Crispy Chickpea Salad

Serves 6 / Prep time: 15 minutes / Cook time: 40 minutes

Crispy chickpeas make a delightful snack and are also one of my favorite ways to add a punch of protein to this healthy and fun main-course salad.

1 (15-ounce) can chickpeas, drained and rinsed

1 tablespoon olive oil

1½ tablespoons barbecue rub

2 heads romaine lettuce, chopped

1 cup halved cherry tomatoes

1 red bell pepper, seeded and chopped

½ cup frozen corn, thawed

4 scallions, chopped

⅓ cup crumbled goat cheese

¾ cup ranch dressing

2 avocados, pitted, peeled, and diced

1. Preheat the oven to 400°F. Line a rimmed baking sheet with parchment paper.

2. In a medium bowl, combine the chickpeas, olive oil, and barbecue rub and toss to coat. Arrange the chickpeas in a single layer on the baking sheet and roast for 30 to 40 minutes, stirring halfway through, until crispy and brown. Let them cool slightly.

3. In a large bowl, toss the romaine, cherry tomatoes, bell pepper, corn, scallions, and goat cheese with the ranch dressing. Top with the chickpeas and avocado.

MAKE AHEAD: Store the roasted chickpeas in an airtight container in the refrigerator for up to 4 days.

Per serving: Calories: 375; Total fat: 28g; Carbohydrates: 28g; Fiber: 12g; Protein: 10g; Sodium: 852mg

Soups and Stews

Creamy Mushroom Soup

Serves 6 / Prep time: 10 minutes / Cook time: 30 minutes

This rich, creamy soup is pure comfort food. If you are pressed for time, you can buy precut mushrooms and onions and jarred minced garlic.

2 tablespoons olive oil

1 pound button and/or cremini mushrooms, sliced

1 large onion, chopped

4 garlic cloves, minced

1 teaspoon dried thyme or 1 tablespoon chopped fresh thyme

4 cups vegetable broth

3 ounces cream cheese, cubed

1 cup half-and-half

Salt and black pepper

1. In a large pot, warm the olive oil over medium heat. Add the mushrooms, onion, garlic, and thyme and sauté until the mushrooms have released most of their liquid, about 8 minutes.

2. Add the vegetable broth and cream cheese and cook until the cream cheese melts, about 5 minutes.

3. Lower the heat to medium-low and stir in the half-and-half. Season with salt and pepper and simmer, stirring, until heated through, about 15 minutes.

MAKE AHEAD: Store this soup in an airtight container in the refrigerator for up to 4 days or in the freezer for up to 2 months.

Per serving: Calories: 177; Total fat: 14g; Carbohydrates: 9g; Fiber: 1g; Protein: 5g; Sodium: 510mg

Tomato-Basil Soup

Serves 6 / Prep time: 10 minutes / Cook time: 1 hour 5 minutes

You can use a countertop blender to blend this soup in batches, but be careful not to overfill it. Remove the cap from the center of the blender lid and hold a dish towel over the hole to allow steam to escape while blending.

1 tablespoon olive oil

1 large onion, finely chopped

1 tablespoon minced garlic

2 cups vegetable broth

1 (28-ounce) can whole peeled tomatoes, undrained

1 (6-ounce) can tomato paste

2 cups chopped fresh basil

½ teaspoon red pepper flakes

Salt and black pepper

½ cup unsweetened plant-based milk of choice

1. In a large pot, warm the olive oil over medium heat. Add the onion and sauté for 10 minutes. Add the garlic and sauté for 1 minute more.

2. Add the vegetable broth, tomatoes with their juices, tomato paste, basil, and red pepper flakes, stir, and bring the mixture to a boil.

3. Lower the heat to medium-low and simmer for 40 minutes. Season the soup with salt and pepper.

4. Using an immersion blender, blend the soup to the desired consistency.

5. Lower the heat to low, stir in the milk, and cook until heated through, about 10 minutes.

MAKE AHEAD: Store this soup in an airtight container in the refrigerator for up to 4 days or in the freezer for up to 3 months.

Per serving: Calories: 94; Total fat: 3g; Carbohydrates: 15g; Fiber: 3g; Protein: 4g; Sodium: 554mg

Spicy Tortellini Soup

Serves 6 / Prep time: 15 minutes / Cook time: 15 minutes

When you need a dinner that you can throw together in a flash, this soup is just what you are looking for. Omit the red pepper flakes if you are serving it to little ones.

1 tablespoon olive oil

1 onion, diced

1 celery stalk, diced

1 carrot, peeled and diced

1 teaspoon minced garlic

1 teaspoon red pepper flakes

¾ teaspoon dried thyme

5 cups vegetable broth

5 ounces baby spinach

1 cup grated vegetarian Parmesan cheese

8 ounces fresh cheese tortellini

1. In a large pot, warm the olive oil over medium-high heat. Add the onion, celery, and carrot and sauté until tender, about 6 minutes. Add the garlic, red pepper flakes, and thyme and sauté for 1 more minute.

2. Add the broth, stir, and bring to a boil. Lower the heat to medium-low, add the spinach, and simmer until it is wilted, about 3 minutes.

3. Add the Parmesan and cook, stirring, until melted.

4. Raise the heat to medium-high and bring the soup to a boil. Add the tortellini and cook until tender, 2 to 5 minutes. Serve immediately.

MAKE AHEAD: Store this soup, without the tortellini, in an airtight container in the refrigerator for up to 5 days. Add the pasta to the simmering broth 2 to 5 minutes before serving.

Per serving: Calories: 204; Total fat: 8g; Carbohydrates: 28g; Fiber: 2g; Protein: 7g; Sodium: 917mg

Roasted Red Pepper and Tomato Soup

Serves 6 / Prep time: 10 minutes / Cook time: 40 minutes

I grew up eating canned tomato soup, and even so, I thought it was such a treat. This version from scratch is all grown up and perfect for dipping a grilled cheese sandwich.

1 tablespoon olive oil

2 roasted red peppers, chopped

1 medium onion, chopped

1 tablespoon minced garlic

1½ cups vegetable broth

1 (28-ounce) can fire-roasted tomatoes, undrained

2 tablespoons tomato paste

1 teaspoon smoked paprika

½ teaspoon red pepper flakes

Salt and black pepper

½ cup unsweetened plant-based milk of choice

1. In a large pot, warm the olive oil over medium heat. Add the roasted red peppers, onion, and garlic and sauté for 10 minutes.

2. Add the vegetable broth, tomatoes with their juices, tomato paste, paprika, and red pepper flakes, stir to combine, and bring the mixture to a boil. Season it with salt and pepper.

3. Lower the heat to medium-low and simmer for 25 minutes. Remove the soup from the heat. Using an immersion blender, puree it until smooth.

4. Return the pot to the heat, add the milk, and cook, stirring, until heated through, about 5 minutes.

MAKE AHEAD: Store this soup in an airtight container in the refrigerator for up to 5 days.

Per serving: Calories: 82; Total fat: 3g; Carbohydrates: 12g; Fiber: 4g; Protein: 2g; Sodium: 642mg

Broccoli Cheese Soup

Serves 6 / Prep time: 10 minutes / Cook time: 15 minutes

Prepare a pot of this soup on Sunday and enjoy an energizing meal for the rest of the week. For a thicker consistency, mix 2 tablespoons flour with 2 tablespoons water and whisk in at the end.

2 tablespoons olive oil

1 onion, diced

2 celery stalks, finely chopped

1 teaspoon minced garlic

1 pound broccoli florets, chopped

3 cups vegetable broth

¼ teaspoon cayenne pepper

Salt and black pepper

1 cup half-and-half

8 ounces shredded cheddar cheese

1. In a large pot, warm the olive oil over medium heat. Add the onion and celery and sauté for 5 minutes. Add the garlic and sauté for 1 minute more.

2. Add the broccoli, broth, and cayenne pepper and bring the mixture to a boil. Season it with salt and pepper.

3. Lower the heat to medium-low, cover, and simmer until the broccoli is tender, 8 to 10 minutes. Remove the pot from the heat.

4. Using an immersion blender, puree the soup to the desired consistency.

5. Return the pot to medium-low heat, add the half-and-half and cheese, and cook until the cheese melts.

MAKE AHEAD: Store this soup in an airtight container in the refrigerator for up to 4 days or in the freezer for up to 2 months.

Per serving: Calories: 279; Total fat: 21g; Carbohydrates: 10g; Fiber: 2g; Protein: 13g; Sodium: 624mg

Smoky Cauliflower Soup

Serves 6 / Prep time: 15 minutes / Cook time: 40 minutes

I have a soft spot for smoked cheeses and couldn't adore this soup more. It has such rich flavors and a creamy texture. When I am in the mood for a little texture, I sprinkle it with spiced pumpkin seeds.

2 tablespoons olive oil

1 large head cauliflower, cut into florets

1 onion, diced

1 russet potato, peeled and diced

1 teaspoon minced garlic

½ teaspoon dried thyme

½ teaspoon dried rosemary

4 cups vegetable broth

4 ounces smoked Gouda cheese, shredded

Salt and black pepper

1. In a large pot, warm the olive oil over low heat. Add the cauliflower, onion, potato, garlic, thyme, and rosemary, cover, and cook for 5 minutes.

2. Increase the heat to medium-high, add the broth, and bring the mixture to a boil. Lower the heat to medium-low and simmer, stirring occasionally, until the vegetables are tender, about 30 minutes.

3. Remove the pot from the heat. Using an immersion blender, puree the soup until very smooth.

4. Return the pot to medium-low heat, add the shredded cheese, and cook until the cheese melts, about 5 minutes. Season the soup with salt and pepper.

MAKE AHEAD: Store this soup in an airtight container in the refrigerator for up to 2 days or in the freezer for up to 2 months.

Per serving: Calories: 184; Total fat: 11g; Carbohydrates: 15g; Fiber: 4g; Protein: 9g; Sodium: 654mg

Potato Cheese Soup

Serves 6 / Prep time: 15 minutes / Cook time: 30 minutes

I often crave comfort food, so this has become a staple in my house. I like to only partially blend it so there are still some chunks of potato.

1 pound russet potatoes

2 tablespoons unsalted butter

1 small onion, diced

1 teaspoon minced garlic

1¼ cups milk

1¼ cups vegetable broth

4 ounces sharp cheddar cheese, shredded

¼ teaspoon cayenne pepper

Salt and black pepper

1. Pierce the potatoes all over with a fork and microwave them on high for 11 minutes, flipping them halfway through. (Alternatively, bake them at 400°F for 1 hour, or until tender.) Let the potatoes cool slightly, then peel and coarsely chop them.

2. In a large pot, melt the butter over medium heat. Add the onion and sauté for 4 minutes. Add the garlic and sauté for 1 minute more.

3. Add the potatoes, milk, and broth and bring the mixture to a boil. Lower the heat to medium-low, cover, and simmer for 10 minutes.

4. Remove the pot from the heat. Using an immersion blender, puree the soup to your desired consistency.

5. Add the cheese and cayenne pepper and cook, stirring frequently, until the cheese melts, about 3 minutes. Season the soup with salt and pepper.

MAKE AHEAD: Store this soup in an airtight container in the refrigerator for up to 4 days.

Per serving: Calories: 183; Total fat: 11g; Carbohydrates: 16g; Fiber: 2g; Protein: 6g; Sodium: 321mg

Fall Vegetable and Wild Rice Soup

Serves 6 / Prep time: 15 minutes / Cook time: 1 hour

I like to serve this soup with warm crusty bread to soak up all of the delicious juices. For a richer soup, use half-and-half or canned coconut milk instead of plain milk.

1 tablespoon olive oil

1 onion, diced

3 carrots, peeled and chopped

2 cups (¼-inch) cubes butternut squash

5 ounces sliced button or cremini mushrooms

1 garlic clove, minced

1 teaspoon dried thyme

1 cup wild rice

6 cups vegetable broth

1 cup unsweetened plant-based milk of choice

Salt and black pepper

1. In a large pot, warm the olive oil over medium heat. Add the onion, carrots, and squash and sauté for 5 minutes. Add the mushrooms, garlic, and thyme and sauté for another 5 minutes.

2. Add the wild rice and broth and bring the mixture to a boil. Lower the heat to medium-low, cover, and simmer until the rice is tender, 45 minutes.

3. Add the milk and stir to combine. Season the soup with salt and pepper and cook until warmed through, about 5 more minutes.

MAKE AHEAD: Store this soup in an airtight container in the refrigerator for up to 3 days.

Per serving: Calories: 197; Total fat: 3g; Carbohydrates: 38g; Fiber: 6g; Protein: 7g; Sodium: 708mg

Green Goddess Soup

Serves 6 / Prep time: 15 minutes / Cook time: 42 minutes

This easy soup is one of the most delicious ways I know of to add greens to your diet. The potato makes it rich and creamy without the need to add dairy.

2 tablespoons olive oil

1 medium onion, finely chopped

Salt and black pepper

2 teaspoons minced garlic

6 cups vegetable broth

6 cups chopped broccoli

1 russet potato, peeled and chopped

6 ounces spinach, roughly chopped

¼ cup chopped fresh basil

½ teaspoon red pepper flakes

2 tablespoons freshly squeezed lemon juice

1. In a large pot, warm the oil over medium-high heat. Add the onion, season it with salt and pepper, and sauté until tender, about 7 minutes. Add the garlic and sauté for 1 more minute.

2. Add the broth, broccoli, and potato, cover, and cook for 30 minutes. Add the spinach, basil, and red pepper flakes and cook, stirring, until the spinach is wilted, about 4 more minutes.

3. Remove the pot from the heat. Using an immersion blender, puree the soup. Stir in the lemon juice.

MAKE-AHEAD: Store this soup in an airtight container in the refrigerator for up to 3 days.

Per serving: Calories: 122; Total fat: 5g; Carbohydrates: 16g; Fiber: 3g; Protein: 4g; Sodium: 694mg

Creamy Pumpkin Soup

Serves 6 / Prep time: 15 minutes / Cook time: 1 hour 7 minutes

Pumpkin soup is a fall tradition, and it doesn't get any better than this creamy version. The maple syrup provides a smooth sweetness that never fails to delight.

1 (1½-pound) pumpkin, peeled, seeded, and cut into 1-inch cubes

2 tablespoons olive oil, divided, plus more to serve

1 onion, chopped

1 teaspoon minced garlic

4 cups vegetable broth

2 tablespoons maple syrup

½ teaspoon ground cinnamon

Salt and black pepper

½ cup half-and-half

3 tablespoons roasted pumpkin seeds

1. Preheat the oven to 375°F. Line a rimmed baking sheet with parchment paper.

2. Toss the pumpkin with 1 tablespoon olive oil and spread it out in a single layer on the prepared baking sheet. Roast for 50 minutes, or until tender.

3. In a large pot, warm the remaining 1 tablespoon olive oil over medium heat. Add the onion and sauté for 6 minutes. Add the garlic and sauté for 1 minute more. Add the pumpkin, broth, maple syrup, and cinnamon and stir to combine. Season the soup with salt and pepper and cook for 10 minutes.

4. Remove the pot from the heat. Using an immersion blender, puree the soup until smooth.

5. Return the pot to low heat, stir in the half-and-half, and cook until heated through. Garnish with a drizzle of olive oil, a few grinds of black pepper, and the pumpkin seeds.

MAKE AHEAD: Store this soup in an airtight container in the refrigerator for up to 5 days.

Per serving: Calories: 171; Total fat: 11g; Carbohydrates: 17g; Fiber: 1g; Protein: 4g; Sodium: 452mg

Easy Ramen

Serves 6 / Prep time: 10 minutes / Cook time: 10 minutes

When you are looking for a quick and easy meal, this simple ramen never fails to hit the spot. A sprinkle of scallions and sesame seeds and a drizzle of sriracha would finish it off nicely.

1 tablespoon toasted sesame oil

1 tablespoon grated fresh ginger

1 teaspoon minced garlic

1 cup shredded carrots

8 ounces sliced button or cremini mushrooms

4 cups vegetable broth

1 (13½-ounce) can unsweetened coconut milk

2 tablespoons soy sauce

6 ounces ramen noodles

Salt and black pepper

1. In a large pot, warm the sesame oil over medium-high heat. Add the ginger and garlic and sauté for 1 minute. Add the carrots and mushrooms and sauté for 4 minutes. Add the broth, coconut milk, and soy sauce and bring to a boil.

2. Remove the pot from the heat and add the ramen noodles. Cover the pot and let it sit until the noodles are tender, 3 to 4 minutes. Season the soup with salt and pepper.

MAKE AHEAD: Store this soup, without the noodles, in an airtight container in the refrigerator for up to 4 days. Add the noodles to the simmering broth and let them soften before serving.

Per serving: Calories: 206; Total fat: 16g; Carbohydrates: 14g; Fiber: 2g; Protein: 4g; Sodium: 765mg

Veggie Noodle Soup

Serves 6 / Prep time: 10 minutes / Cook time: 36 minutes

Few foods comfort as much as a warm bowl of noodle soup. This simple recipe is one I turn to whenever I'm feeling under the weather.

1 tablespoon olive oil

1 large onion, chopped

4 celery stalks, chopped

3 medium
carrots, chopped

2 teaspoons
minced garlic

1 cup dry white wine
or water

5 cups vegetable broth

2 bay leaves

1 teaspoon dried thyme

Salt and black pepper

1 cup medium
egg noodles

1. In a large pot, warm the oil over medium heat. Add the onion, celery, and carrots and sauté for 10 minutes. Add the garlic and sauté for 1 more minute. Add the wine, bring the soup to a boil, and cook for 5 minutes.

2. Lower the heat to medium-low and add the broth, bay leaves, and thyme. Season the soup with salt and pepper, cover, and cook for 10 minutes.

3. Raise the heat to medium-high and bring the soup back to a boil. Add the noodles and cook until the noodles are tender, 6 to 10 minutes. Remove the bay leaves.

MAKE AHEAD: Store this soup, without the noodles, in an airtight container in the refrigerator for up to 5 days or in the freezer for up to 3 months. Add the noodles to the simmering broth 6 to 10 minutes before serving.

Per serving: Calories: 124; Total fat: 3g; Carbohydrates: 16g; Fiber: 2g; Protein: 3g; Sodium: 594mg

Taco Pasta Soup

Serves 6 / Prep time: 15 minutes / Cook time: 17 minutes

Hearty soups like this one are the most requested form of soup at our house. We like to top each bowl with traditional taco fixings such as diced avocado, shredded cheese, and a dollop of sour cream.

1 tablespoon olive oil

1 large onion, chopped

1 teaspoon minced garlic

6 cups vegetable broth

1 (10-ounce) can diced tomatoes with green chiles, undrained

¼ cup taco seasoning

Salt and black pepper

2 cups elbow macaroni

1 (15-ounce) can pinto beans, drained and rinsed

1 cup frozen corn, thawed

1. In a large pot, warm the olive oil over medium heat. Add the onion and sauté for 7 minutes. Add the garlic and sauté for 1 minute longer. Add the broth, tomatoes and chiles with their juices, and taco seasoning and stir to combine. Season the soup with salt and pepper, raise the heat to high, and bring it to a boil.

2. Add the pasta and cook until tender, about 5 minutes.

3. Lower the heat to medium-low, add the pinto beans and corn, and cook until warm throughout, about 5 minutes.

MAKE AHEAD: Store this soup, without the pasta, in an airtight container in the refrigerator for up to 3 days or in the freezer for up to 3 months. Add the pasta to the simmering broth 5 minutes before serving.

Per serving: Calories: 291; Total fat: 4g; Carbohydrates: 55g; Fiber: 6g; Protein: 11g; Sodium: 1201mg

Sweet Potato Dal

Serves 6 / Prep time: 10 minutes / Cook time: 40 minutes

Garam masala is an Indian spice blend that gives this simple dish its bold flavors. If you don't have it, use 2½ teaspoons ground cumin and ¼ teaspoon ground allspice. The flavors won't be quite as intense, but it will still be delicious.

1 tablespoon coconut oil

1 onion, diced

1 tablespoon minced fresh ginger

1 tablespoon garam masala

2 sweet potatoes, peeled and diced

1 cup red lentils

4 cups vegetable broth

1 cup canned unsweetened coconut milk

5 ounces baby spinach

Salt and black pepper

1. In a large pot, warm the coconut oil over medium heat. Add the onion, ginger, and garam masala and sauté for 5 minutes. Add the sweet potatoes and sauté for 5 minutes.

2. Add the lentils and vegetable broth and bring to a boil. Lower the heat to medium-low and simmer until the lentils are cooked and the sweet potatoes are tender, 20 to 25 minutes.

3. Add the coconut milk and spinach and cook until the spinach wilts and the soup is heated through, about 3 minutes. Season the soup with salt and pepper.

MAKE AHEAD: Store this soup in an airtight container in the refrigerator for up to 3 days.

Per serving: Calories: 265; Total fat: 11g; Carbohydrates: 34g; Fiber: 6g; Protein: 10g; Sodium: 487mg

Moroccan-Inspired Vegetable Stew

Serves 6 / Prep time: 15 minutes / Cook time: 55 minutes

Loaded with flavor, this hearty stew is perfect for those cooler months when you need something that will warm you to the bone. Serve it over couscous to make it even more filling.

2 tablespoons olive oil

2 large onions, chopped

1½ teaspoons ground cumin

1 teaspoon ground ginger

½ teaspoon ground coriander

¼ teaspoon smoked paprika

2 cups diced carrots

1 large sweet potato, peeled and chopped

½ head cauliflower, chopped

1 (15-ounce) can chickpeas, drained and rinsed

4 cups vegetable broth

Salt and black pepper

1. In a large pot, warm the olive oil over medium-high heat. Add the onions and sauté for 5 minutes. Add the cumin, ginger, coriander, and smoked paprika and sauté for 1 more minute.

2. Add the carrots, sweet potato, cauliflower, chickpeas, and broth and simmer until the vegetables are tender, about 45 minutes. Season the stew with salt and pepper.

MAKE AHEAD: Store this stew in an airtight container in the refrigerator for up to 3 days.

Per serving: Calories: 197; Total fat: 6g; Carbohydrates: 31g; Fiber: 7g; Protein: 6g; Sodium: 602mg

Curried Lentil Soup

Serves 6 / Prep time: 15 minutes / Cook time: 50 minutes

Lentils are the ultimate budget-friendly protein, but this lentil soup feels like anything but a sacrifice. Serve with a crusty baguette or naan bread for a complete meal.

1 tablespoon olive oil

1 onion, chopped

2 carrots, peeled and diced

2 celery stalks, chopped

1 tablespoon minced fresh ginger

1 teaspoon minced garlic

1½ teaspoons curry powder

½ teaspoon ground cumin

½ teaspoon ground turmeric

Salt and black pepper

1 cup French green lentils, rinsed

6 cups vegetable broth

1. In a large pot, warm the olive oil over medium heat. Add the onion, carrots, and celery and sauté for 7 minutes. Add the ginger, garlic, curry powder, cumin, and turmeric and stir to combine. Season the veggies with salt and pepper and sauté for 1 minute longer.

2. Add the lentils and broth and bring to a boil. Lower the heat to medium-low, cover, and simmer for 40 minutes.

MAKE AHEAD: Store this soup in an airtight container in the refrigerator for up to 3 days.

Per serving: Calories: 133; Total fat: 3g; Carbohydrates: 20g; Fiber: 4g; Protein: 7g; Sodium: 681mg

White Bean Stew

Serves 6 / Prep time: 10 minutes / Cook time: 44 minutes

This stew is so hearty that all you need is a simple green salad for a side dish. If you like, chopped kale can be used in place of the spinach.

2 tablespoons olive oil

3 medium carrots, peeled and thinly sliced

4 celery stalks, thinly sliced

1 large onion, chopped

1 teaspoon minced garlic

1 (28-ounce) can crushed tomatoes

2 cups vegetable broth

2 (15-ounce) cans cannellini beans, drained and rinsed

Salt and black pepper

2 cups baby spinach

¼ cup chopped fresh basil

1. In a large pot, warm the olive oil over medium heat. Add the carrots, celery, and onion and sauté for 8 minutes. Add the garlic and sauté for 1 more minute.

2. Add the tomatoes and broth and bring to a boil. Lower the heat to medium-low, add the beans, and cook for 30 minutes. Season the soup with salt and pepper.

3. Add the spinach and basil and cook until the spinach wilts, about 3 minutes.

MAKE AHEAD: Store this soup in an airtight container in the refrigerator for up to 4 days.

Per serving: Calories: 177; Total fat: 6g; Carbohydrates: 28g; Fiber: 8g; Protein: 7g; Sodium: 556mg

Chickpea Stew

Serves 6 / Prep time: 10 minutes / Cook time: 35 minutes

Dinners don't get much healthier than this hearty stew. I try to use turmeric whenever I can because of its many health benefits and anti-inflammatory properties.

1 tablespoon olive oil

1 onion, chopped

1 red bell pepper, seeded and chopped

1 tablespoon minced fresh ginger

1 teaspoon minced garlic

2 teaspoons ground cumin

2 teaspoons ground turmeric

2 (15-ounce) cans chickpeas, drained and rinsed

1 (14½-ounce) can diced tomatoes, undrained

Salt and black pepper

1. In a large pot, warm the olive oil over medium-high heat. Add the onion and bell pepper and sauté for 8 minutes. Add the ginger and garlic and sauté for 1 minute. Add the cumin and turmeric and sauté for 2 minutes more.

2. Lower the heat to medium-low, add the chickpeas and tomatoes with their juices, and cook until heated through, 20 to 25 minutes. Season the stew with salt and pepper.

MAKE AHEAD: Store this stew in an airtight container in the refrigerator for up to 4 days.

Per serving: Calories: 180; Total fat: 5g; Carbohydrates: 28g; Fiber: 8g; Protein: 8g; Sodium: 355mg

Corn Chowder

Serves 6 / Prep time: 15 minutes / Cook time: 28 minutes

When fresh corn is at the height of its season, this chowder is something special. But don't worry, frozen corn is a good alternative for the rest of the year.

1 tablespoon olive oil

1 onion, diced

2 celery stalks, diced

1 pound Yukon Gold potatoes, peeled and cut into ½-inch cubes

4 cups vegetable broth

4 cups corn, fresh or frozen

½ teaspoon ground chipotle chile

Salt and black pepper

1. In a large pot, warm the olive oil over medium-high heat. Add the onion and celery and sauté until softened, about 6 minutes. Add the potatoes and broth and bring to a boil.

2. Lower the heat to medium-low, cover, and simmer for 10 minutes.

3. Remove the pot from the heat. Using an immersion blender, puree the soup to the desired consistency.

4. Return the soup to medium-low heat. Add the corn and ground chipotle chile, stir to combine, and cook until warm throughout, about 12 minutes. Season the chowder with salt and pepper.

MAKE AHEAD: Store this soup in an airtight container in the refrigerator for up to 4 days.

Per serving: Calories: 188; Total fat: 3g; Carbohydrates: 39g; Fiber: 4g; Protein: 5g; Sodium: 460mg

Roasted Garlic Soup

Serves 6 / Prep time: 15 minutes / Cook time: 1 hour 55 minutes

Garlic lovers, unite! This creamy soup packs a punch of garlicky goodness. Serve with a squeeze of fresh lemon juice and be prepared for a party in your mouth.

6 heads garlic

2 tablespoons avocado oil

2 tablespoons unsalted butter

2 medium onions, thinly sliced

1 teaspoon dried thyme

1 teaspoon minced garlic

3½ cups vegetable broth

⅓ cup half-and-half

½ cup grated vegetarian Parmesan cheese

Salt and black pepper

1. Preheat the oven to 425°F.

2. Slice the top ½ inch or so off the garlic heads, enough to expose the cloves. Place the garlic heads in a baking dish. Drizzle them with the oil and cover the baking dish with aluminum foil. Roast for 45 minutes.

3. Remove the foil and roast for 15 minutes more, or until the garlic is golden brown. Let the garlic cool, then squeeze the cloves from the skins.

4. In a large pot, melt the butter over medium-high heat. Add the onions and thyme and sauté for 9 minutes. Add the roasted garlic and sauté for another 5 minutes.

5. Add the minced garlic and vegetable broth and bring the mixture to a boil, stirring occasionally. Lower the heat to medium-low, cover, and simmer for 35 minutes.

6. Add the half-and-half and Parmesan and cook until the cheese melts, about 5 minutes. Season the soup with salt and pepper.

MAKE AHEAD: Store the roasted garlic in an airtight container in the refrigerator for up to 1 week or in the freezer for up to 3 months.

Per serving: Calories: 160; Total fat: 11g; Carbohydrates: 13g; Fiber: 1g; Protein: 2g; Sodium: 488mg

Handhelds

Southwestern Black Bean Wraps

Serves 4 / Prep time: 10 minutes / Cook time: 15 minutes

These wraps come together in less time than it would take you to get take-out burritos. If you are in the mood to add something cheesy, a sharp cheddar does nicely here.

2 tablespoons olive oil, divided

½ cup diced red onion

4 cups chopped spinach

1 cup frozen corn, thawed

1 (15-ounce) can black beans, drained and rinsed

½ cup salsa

Salt and black pepper

2 tablespoons chopped fresh cilantro

½ cup guacamole

4 large flour tortillas

1. In a large skillet, warm 1 tablespoon oil over medium heat. Add the onion and sauté for 5 minutes. Add the spinach and sauté until wilted, about 1 minute. Add the corn, black beans, and salsa, stir, and cook until heated through, about 3 minutes. Season with salt and pepper. Transfer to a large bowl and stir in the cilantro; reserve the skillet.

2. Spread the guacamole on each tortilla. Top with the black bean mixture. Tuck the sides in and roll the tortillas up, then secure with toothpicks.

3. Wipe out the skillet and warm the remaining 1 tablespoon oil over medium heat. Add the wraps to the skillet, seam-side down, and cook until golden brown, about 2 minutes per side.

MAKE AHEAD: These wraps can be made up to 1 day ahead of time, covered tightly with plastic wrap, and refrigerated, then browned in a skillet when ready to serve.

Per serving: Calories: 460; Total fat: 17g; Carbohydrates: 68g; Fiber: 13g; Protein: 13g; Sodium: 881mg

Chickpea Salad Wraps

Serves 4 / Prep time: 10 minutes

These wraps tip their hat to traditional tuna salad while remaining deliciously vegetarian. For a fun twist, I like to add ⅓ cup chopped sun-dried tomatoes, 1 tablespoon capers, and 1 tablespoon chopped fresh parsley.

1 (15-ounce) can chickpeas, drained and rinsed

1 avocado, pitted, peeled, and mashed

2 tablespoons mayonnaise

1 tablespoon Dijon mustard

1 tablespoon apple cider vinegar

3 celery stalks, finely chopped

½ red onion, finely diced

2 teaspoons dried dill or 2 tablespoons chopped fresh dill

Salt and black pepper

4 medium flour tortillas

1 cup baby spinach

1. In a medium bowl, combine the chickpeas and avocado. Using the back of a fork or a potato masher, partially mash the chickpeas.

2. Add the mayonnaise, Dijon mustard, and apple cider vinegar and stir until well combined. Add the celery, red onion, and dill, season with salt and pepper, and stir to combine.

3. Spread the chickpea salad mixture on each tortilla and top with the spinach. Tuck the sides in and roll the tortillas up, then secure with toothpicks.

MAKE AHEAD: You can make the chickpea salad up to 4 days ahead and store it in an airtight container in the refrigerator, then make the wraps when ready to serve. Alternatively, these wraps can be wrapped tightly in plastic wrap or parchment paper and refrigerated for up to 2 days.

Per serving: Calories: 353; Total fat: 17g; Carbohydrates: 43g; Fiber: 9g; Protein: 9g; Sodium: 539mg

Garden Vegetable Wraps

Serves 4 / Prep time: 10 minutes

These healthy wraps come together in a flash and are packed with delicious ingredients that will leave you feeling great. For a little extra protein, add cooked or canned beans, crumbled steamed tempeh, or your favorite chopped nuts.

½ cup hummus

4 large sandwich wraps

2 cups chopped romaine lettuce

1½ cups shredded purple cabbage

1 red bell pepper, seeded and diced

¼ cup chopped cherry tomatoes

¼ cup alfalfa sprouts

2 avocados, pitted, peeled, and sliced

1. Spread the hummus on each wrap. Top with the romaine, cabbage, bell pepper, cherry tomatoes, sprouts, and avocado.

2. Tuck the sides in and roll the wraps up, then secure with toothpicks.

MAKE AHEAD: Store the vegetables in an airtight container in the refrigerator for up to 4 days. Wait to cut the avocado until just before preparing the wraps.

Per serving: Calories: 416; Total fat: 20g; Carbohydrates: 51g; Fiber: 12g; Protein: 11g; Sodium: 706mg

Margherita Sandwiches

Serves 4 / Prep time: 10 minutes / Cook time: 10 minutes

This kid-friendly recipe is what I make on those nights when I need to get dinner on the table in less than 20 minutes. Serve it with a simple salad of peppery arugula on the side.

¼ cup olive oil

1 teaspoon Italian seasoning

1 teaspoon garlic powder

8 slices bread

¼ cup marinara sauce

6 ounces whole-milk mozzarella cheese, sliced

1 tomato, thinly sliced

12 fresh basil leaves

2 teaspoons balsamic vinegar

1. In a small bowl, mix together the olive oil, Italian seasoning, and garlic powder. Brush the mixture on one side of each slice of bread. Spread the marinara on the other side of each slice of bread. Top the marinara side of 4 bread slices with the mozzarella cheese, sliced tomato, basil, and balsamic vinegar. Place the remaining bread slices on top, oil-side up.

2. Coat a large skillet with cooking spray and set it over medium heat. Add the sandwiches and cook until the cheese melts and the outside is crusty and brown, about 5 minutes per side. You may need to cook them in batches.

MAKE AHEAD: While best fresh, these sandwiches can be assembled up to 1 day ahead, wrapped tightly with plastic wrap, and stored in the refrigerator, then browned in a skillet when ready to serve.

Per serving: Calories: 505; Total fat: 27g; Carbohydrates: 48g; Fiber: 3g; Protein: 18g; Sodium: 785mg

Roasted Red Pepper and Goat Cheese Sandwiches

Serves 4 / Prep time: 15 minutes

This sandwich is one of my go-to lunches and easy dinners. I often serve it with White Bean Salad with Tahini Dressing (page 105) for a satisfying meal.

½ **red onion, thinly sliced**

1 tablespoon balsamic vinegar

2 tablespoons extra-virgin olive oil

2 cups arugula

4 ciabatta rolls, split and toasted

8 ounces goat cheese, softened

2 roasted red peppers, cut into strips

1. In a medium bowl, toss together the onion slices and vinegar and let it stand for 10 minutes. Use a fork or tongs to transfer the onions to a small bowl.

2. Add the olive oil to the balsamic vinegar remaining in the medium bowl, then add the arugula and toss to combine.

3. Spread both halves of the ciabatta rolls with the goat cheese. Layer the bottoms of the rolls with the red peppers, onions, and arugula. Cover with the roll tops.

SUBSTITUTE: Chive cream cheese makes a nice alternative to the goat cheese.

Per serving: Calories: 478; Total fat: 25g; Carbohydrates: 42g; Fiber: 4g; Protein: 20g; Sodium: 810mg

VLT Sandwiches

Serves 4 / Prep time: 15 minutes

VLTs are what I turn to when I need a quick meal that doesn't require a lot of effort. You won't believe how fabulous the smoky homemade "bacon" is here!

¼ cup mayonnaise

8 slices bread, toasted

1 large tomato, sliced

8 leaves romaine lettuce

½ recipe Vegetarian Bacon (page 22)

1. Spread the mayonnaise on the bread slices.

2. Top 4 slices with the tomato, lettuce, and bacon. Top with the remaining slices of bread, mayonnaise-side down.

SUBSTITUTE: To save time, purchased vegetarian bacon can be used. You can find it in the refrigerated section of many grocery stores, often near the produce.

Per serving: Calories: 436; Total fat: 23g; Carbohydrates: 49g; Fiber: 6g; Protein: 10g; Sodium: 592mg

Garlicky Kale Grilled Cheese

Serves 4 / Prep time: 10 minutes / Cook time: 15 minutes

Adding a little kale to this indulgent sandwich makes me feel a bit better about my life decisions. Serve this with Roasted Red Pepper and Tomato Soup (page 62) for a flavor-packed meal.

2 cups shredded kale

⅓ cup chopped sun-dried tomatoes

1 teaspoon minced garlic

4 tablespoons unsalted butter, softened

8 slices bread

8 slices cheddar cheese

¼ cup crumbled feta cheese

1. Coat a large skillet generously with cooking spray and set it over medium heat. Add the kale and sauté until it begins to wilt, about 4 minutes. Add the sun-dried tomatoes and garlic and sauté for 1 minute more. Transfer the mixture to a bowl.

2. Spread the butter on one side of each slice of bread.

3. Wipe the skillet clean with a paper towel, coat it again with cooking spray, and set it over medium heat. Place 4 of the bread slices, buttered-side down, in the skillet and top them with the cheddar cheese, feta, and kale mixture. Top with the remaining 4 slices of bread, buttered-side up, and cook until golden brown, 4 or 5 minutes per side.

MAKE AHEAD: Store the kale filling in an airtight container in the refrigerator for up to 4 days.

Per serving: Calories: 512; Total fat: 29g; Carbohydrates: 48g; Fiber: 3g; Protein: 18g; Sodium: 850mg

Jalapeño Pimento Cheese Panini

Serves 4 / Prep time: 10 minutes / Cook time: 20 minutes

When you are craving bold flavors, this sandwich is absolute perfection. Consider doubling the amount of pimento cheese so you'll have leftovers to serve as a snack later in the week.

4 ounces cream cheese, softened

¼ cup mayonnaise

2 cups shredded sharp cheddar cheese

½ teaspoon minced garlic

1 (4-ounce) jar pimentos, drained

1 jalapeño, seeded and diced

¼ teaspoon smoked paprika

Salt and black pepper

8 bread slices

1. Preheat a panini maker (if using).

2. In a medium bowl, beat the cream cheese and mayonnaise with an electric mixer until smooth. Add the cheddar cheese, garlic, pimentos, jalapeño, and paprika and beat until just combined. Season the mixture with salt and pepper.

3. Spray one side of each slice of bread with cooking spray. Spread the pimento cheese on the non-sprayed sides of 4 bread slices. Top with the remaining 4 bread slices, sprayed-side up.

4. Press the sandwiches in the panini maker until golden brown, 3 to 5 minutes for each sandwich. (Alternatively, coat a skillet with cooking spray and set it over medium-high heat. Place a sandwich in the center of the skillet, place a pot lid on top of the sandwich, and cook until crispy and golden brown, 2 to 3 minutes per side.)

MAKE AHEAD: Store the pimento cheese in an airtight container in the refrigerator for up to 4 days.

Per serving: Calories: 653; Total fat: 41g; Carbohydrates: 48g; Fiber: 3g; Protein: 24g; Sodium: 967mg

Swiss, Mushroom, and Caramelized Onion Sandwiches

Serves 4 / Prep time: 10 minutes / Cook time: 1 hour

Caramelizing onions is a task that takes some time, but it's not hard. I make them on Sundays when I am already in the kitchen doing weekly meal prep.

7 tablespoons unsalted butter, divided

2 onions, thinly sliced

Salt and black pepper

8 ounces button or cremini mushrooms, sliced

8 slices bread

4 slices Swiss cheese

1. In a large skillet, melt 2 tablespoons butter over medium-high heat. Add the onions, season them with salt and pepper, and sauté for 5 minutes. Reduce the heat to low and cook, stirring occasionally, until the onions are golden and caramelized, 35 to 40 minutes. Add water, 1 tablespoon at a time, as needed to prevent burning. Transfer the onions to a bowl.

2. In the same skillet, melt 1 tablespoon butter over medium heat. Add the mushrooms and sauté for 8 minutes.

3. Spread the remaining 4 tablespoons butter on one side of each of the bread slices.

4. Wipe the skillet clean with a paper towel and set it over medium-low heat. Place 4 bread slices, buttered-side down, in the skillet. Layer with the cheese, onions, and mushrooms and top with the remaining bread slices, buttered-side up. Cover and cook until brown, 2 to 3 minutes. Flip the sandwiches and cook until golden on the other side, 2 to 3 minutes.

MAKE AHEAD: Store the sautéed onions and mushrooms in separate airtight containers in the refrigerator for up to 4 days.

Per serving: Calories: 511; Total fat: 28g; Carbohydrates: 51g; Fiber: 4g; Protein: 15g; Sodium: 621mg

Roasted Chickpea Gyros

Serves 6 / Prep time: 15 minutes / Cook time: 1 hour 15 minutes

If you don't have Mediterranean seasoning on hand, a blend of ground cumin, paprika, and garlic powder works nicely here.

1 (15-ounce) can chickpeas, drained and rinsed

1 tablespoon olive oil

1½ tablespoons Mediterranean seasoning

1 cucumber, peeled, seeded, and finely chopped

Salt and black pepper

¾ cup plain Greek yogurt

1 tablespoon freshly squeezed lemon juice

2 teaspoons chopped fresh dill

3 garlic cloves, minced

6 pitas, warmed

3 cups chopped romaine lettuce

⅓ cup thinly sliced red onion

⅓ cup diced tomato

¼ cup crumbled feta cheese

1. Preheat the oven to 400°F. Line a rimmed baking sheet with parchment paper.

2. In a large bowl, mix together the chickpeas, olive oil, and Mediterranean seasoning. Spread out the chickpeas in a single layer on the prepared baking sheet. Roast for 35 to 45 minutes, stirring halfway, until crispy and lightly browned.

3. Meanwhile, to make the tzatziki sauce, pile the cucumbers in a strainer set over a bowl, sprinkle well with salt, and let sit for 30 minutes. Using a clean dish towel, gently squeeze out any excess moisture.

4. In a medium bowl, mix together the cucumber, yogurt, lemon juice, dill, and garlic. Season the tzatziki with salt and pepper and stir to combine.

5. Fill the pitas with the roasted chickpeas, lettuce, onion, tomato, and feta. Drizzle with the tzatziki sauce.

MAKE AHEAD: Store the roasted chickpeas in an airtight container in the refrigerator for up to 4 days.

Per serving: Calories: 305; Total fat: 7g; Carbohydrates: 48g; Fiber: 6g; Protein: 13g; Sodium: 488mg

Tofu Kebabs

Serves 4 / Prep time: 50 minutes / Cook time: 30 minutes

When you need a protein-packed meal, these delicious kebabs fit the bill. Finish them off with a sprinkle of sesame seeds and dip them in Green Goddess Dressing (page 54).

1 (14-ounce) package extra-firm tofu

3 lemons, 2 juiced and 1 cut in half

½ teaspoon smoked paprika

Salt and black pepper

1 large zucchini, sliced

1 medium red onion, cut into quarters

1 large carrot, cut into ribbons

1 teaspoon black sesame seeds

1. Line a plate with a double layer of paper towels. Place the tofu on the plate. Top with another double layer of paper towels and another plate. Place something heavy (such as a few cans of tomatoes) on top and let the tofu drain for 10 minutes.

2. In a small bowl, mix together the lemon juice and smoked paprika and season it with salt and pepper. In a large bowl, combine the tofu, zucchini, onion, and carrot and toss with the lemon juice mixture. Let sit for 30 minutes. If using wooden skewers, soak them in water for 30 minutes.

3. Preheat the oven to 400°F. Line a rimmed baking sheet with parchment paper.

4. Cut the tofu into 1-inch cubes. Thread the tofu and vegetables alternately onto the skewers and arrange them in a single layer on the prepared baking sheet. Place the lemon halves, cut-sides down, on the baking sheet.

5. Bake for 25 to 30 minutes, flipping the skewers halfway through, until tender. Squeeze the lemons over the kebabs and sprinkle them with the black sesame seeds.

MAKE AHEAD: Store the baked kebabs in an airtight container in the refrigerator for up to 4 days.

Per serving: Calories: 153; Total fat: 6g; Carbohydrates: 14g; Fiber: 4g; Protein: 14g; Sodium: 54mg

Vegetarian Reuben

Serves 4 / Prep time: 10 minutes / Cook time: 20 minutes

We used to go to a little restaurant near our home that had the best Reuben sandwiches. This recipe reminds me of it while remaining veg-friendly. Serve with more dill pickles on the side.

8 ounces button or cremini mushrooms, sliced

2 roasted red peppers, diced

¼ cup mayonnaise

3 tablespoons ketchup

3 tablespoons finely minced dill pickles

8 slices rye bread

4 slices Swiss cheese

2 cups sauerkraut

1. Spray a large skillet well with cooking spray and set it over medium-high heat. Add the mushrooms and sauté for 10 minutes. Add the red peppers and sauté for another 2 minutes.

2. In a small bowl, mix together the mayonnaise, ketchup, and dill pickles.

3. Spread the mayonnaise mixture equally on one side of each bread slice. Top 4 slices of the bread with the mushroom mixture, cheese, and sauerkraut. Cover with the remaining slices of bread, mayonnaise-side down.

4. Wipe the skillet clean with a paper towel and set over medium heat. Coat both sides of the sandwiches well with cooking spray and cook until golden brown, 3 to 4 minutes per side.

MAKE AHEAD: Store the mushroom mixture and mayonnaise mixture in separate airtight containers in the refrigerator for up to 4 days.

Per serving: Calories: 387; Total fat: 18g; Carbohydrates: 43g; Fiber: 8g; Protein: 14g; Sodium: 1775mg

French Dip

Serves 4 / Prep time: 10 minutes / Cook time: 35 minutes

The secret to this sandwich is making sure the mushroom mixture is well drained before you add it to the bread. For an extra punch of flavor, add a touch of horseradish mayonnaise.

2 tablespoons olive oil, divided

2 onions, thinly sliced

1 teaspoon minced garlic

1 pound portobellos mushroom caps, sliced

2 cups vegetable broth

1½ tablespoons soy sauce

1 tablespoon vegan or vegetarian Worcestershire sauce

1 teaspoon dried rosemary, crushed

½ teaspoon dried thyme

Salt and black pepper

4 hoagie rolls, split

4 slices provolone cheese

1. In a large skillet, warm 1 tablespoon oil over medium-high heat. Add the onions and sauté for 10 minutes. Lower the heat to medium-low, add the garlic and mushroom slices, and sauté for 10 minutes.

2. Add the broth, soy sauce, Worcestershire sauce, rosemary, and thyme and stir to scrape up any brown bits on the bottom of the pan. Season with salt and pepper.

3. Raise the heat to high, bring to a boil, and cook until the liquid is slightly reduced, about 5 minutes.

4. Preheat the broiler.

5. Brush the insides of the hoagie rolls with the remaining 1 tablespoon oil, place them on a rimmed baking sheet, and broil until lightly browned, about 3 minutes.

6. Strain the mushrooms in a colander placed over a bowl.

7. Divide the mushrooms among the hoagie rolls and top each with a slice of cheese. Broil until the cheese melts, about 3 minutes. Pour the mushroom juices into individual ramekins and serve alongside for dipping.

MAKE AHEAD: Store the mushroom mixture and dipping juices in separate airtight containers in the refrigerator for up to 4 days.

Per serving: Calories: 391; Total fat: 14g; Carbohydrates: 49g; Fiber: 4g; Protein: 16g; Sodium: 1229mg

BBQ Jackfruit Sandwiches

Serves 6 / Prep time: 15 minutes / Cook time: 23 minutes

My husband is a die-hard carnivore and mistook leftover BBQ jackfruit for chicken one night. I couldn't help but laugh when he thanked me for making him such a delicious chicken sandwich.

1 (28-ounce) can green jackfruit in brine, drained and rinsed

2 tablespoons olive oil

1 large onion, diced

2 cups barbecue sauce

1 cup vegetable broth

¼ cup mayonnaise

3 tablespoons freshly squeezed lime juice

1 (8-ounce) package coleslaw mix

¼ cup chopped fresh cilantro

Salt and black pepper

6 buns, toasted

1. Using 2 forks, shred the jackfruit.

2. In a skillet, warm the olive oil over medium heat. Add the onion and sauté for 5 minutes. Add the jackfruit and cook, stirring occasionally, for 7 minutes. Add the BBQ sauce and broth, stir to combine, and bring to a boil. Lower the heat to medium-low and simmer, stirring occasionally, for 10 minutes.

3. In a small bowl, mix together the mayonnaise and lime juice. In a large bowl, mix together the coleslaw and cilantro, add the mayonnaise mixture, and stir to combine. Season with salt and pepper and toss again to combine.

4. Spoon the BBQ jackfruit and coleslaw onto the buns and serve.

MAKE AHEAD: Store the BBQ jackfruit in an airtight container in the refrigerator for up to 4 days.

Per serving: Calories: 481; Total fat: 15g; Carbohydrates: 79g; Fiber: 6g; Protein: 9g; Sodium: 2232mg

Buffalo Tempeh Sliders

Serves 6 / Prep time: 10 minutes / Cook time: 30 minutes

It always amazes me how simple buffalo sauce can pack so much punchy flavor. Top these with a coleslaw like the one from the BBQ Jackfruit Sandwiches (page 100).

1 (1-pound) package tempeh

¾ cup unsweetened plant-based milk of choice

1 teaspoon freshly squeezed lemon juice

¾ cup all-purpose flour

Salt and black pepper

2 tablespoons olive oil

½ cup buffalo sauce

6 slider buns

1. Place a steamer basket in a large pot, pour in 2 inches of water, and bring it to a boil over high heat. Lower the heat to medium, add the tempeh, cover, and steam for 10 minutes. Cut the tempeh in half lengthwise and then into patties that fit the slider buns.

2. In a shallow bowl, mix together the milk and lemon juice and let it sit for 5 minutes. Put the flour in another shallow bowl and season it with salt and pepper.

3. Dredge each tempeh patty in the flour mixture, then in the milk mixture, and then in the flour mixture again. Put the patties on a plate.

4. In a large skillet, warm the olive oil over medium heat. Place the patties in the skillet and cook until golden, about 8 minutes per side.

5. In a small saucepan, warm the buffalo sauce over medium heat. Brush the tempeh patties with the sauce, place them on the slider buns, and serve.

MAKE AHEAD: Make the tempeh patties up to 4 days ahead and store them in an airtight container in the refrigerator.

Per serving: Calories: 372; Total fat: 14g; Carbohydrates: 42g; Fiber: 11g; Protein: 23g; Sodium: 775mg

CHAPTER SEVEN

Beans and Grains

Smoky Black Beans with Turmeric Rice

Serves 4 / Prep time: 10 minutes / Cook time: 1 hour

Rice and beans are classic vegetarian fare, and this fun twist is always a welcome addition at our table. Serve it with a green salad for a complete meal.

2 tablespoons olive oil, divided

2 onions, diced, divided

1¾ cups vegetable broth

1 cup brown rice, rinsed

1 teaspoon ground turmeric

1 teaspoon ground cumin

Salt and black pepper

1 (15-ounce) can black beans, drained and rinsed

1 tablespoon garlic powder

1½ teaspoons smoked paprika

1. In a saucepan, warm 1 tablespoon olive oil over medium-high heat. Add half of the onions and sauté for 5 minutes. Add the broth, rice, turmeric, and cumin and bring to a boil. Season with salt and pepper.

2. Lower the heat to medium-low, cover, and cook for 40 minutes. Remove the pan from the heat and let it sit, covered, for 10 minutes.

3. In another saucepan, warm the remaining 1 tablespoon oil over medium-high heat. Add the remaining onions and sauté until softened, about 5 minutes. Add the black beans, garlic powder, and smoked paprika and cook until heated through, about 5 minutes. Season the bean mixture with salt and pepper.

4. Spoon the rice onto plates and top it with the beans.

MAKE AHEAD: Store the rice and beans in an airtight container in the refrigerator for up to 3 days.

Per serving: Calories: 357; Total fat: 64g; Carbohydrates: 64g; Fiber: 12g; Protein: 11g; Sodium: 292mg

White Bean Salad with Tahini Dressing

Serves 6 / Prep time: 15 minutes

A garlicky lemon-tahini sauce perfectly complements mild white beans, and pumpkin seeds add the perfect crunch.

2 tablespoons extra-virgin olive oil

2 tablespoons tahini

2 tablespoons freshly squeezed lemon juice

1 teaspoon minced garlic

Salt and black pepper

2 (15-ounce) cans cannellini or navy beans, drained and rinsed

1 red bell pepper, seeded and diced

½ cup shredded carrots

½ cup diced celery

2 tablespoons chopped fresh parsley

½ cup salted pumpkin seeds

1. In a small bowl, whisk together the olive oil, tahini, lemon juice, and garlic. Season the dressing to taste with salt and pepper.

2. In a large bowl, combine the beans, red bell pepper, carrots, celery, and parsley. Toss with the dressing and top with the pumpkin seeds.

MAKE AHEAD: Store this salad in an airtight container in the refrigerator for up to 4 days.

Per serving: Calories: 255; Total fat: 13g; Carbohydrates: 25g; Fiber: 8g; Protein: 11g; Sodium: 94mg

Falafel Bowls

Serves 4 / Prep time: 30 minutes / Cook time: 5 minutes

Bowls are the best way to enjoy these tasty little morsels. Top with the tzatziki sauce from the Roasted Chickpea Gyros (page 95) and garnish with crumbled pita chips.

1 (15-ounce) can chickpeas, drained and rinsed

1 cup chopped fresh parsley or cilantro

2 tablespoons tahini

2 teaspoons minced garlic

¼ cup all-purpose flour

1½ teaspoons baking powder

1 teaspoon ground cumin

Salt and black pepper

6 cups shredded romaine lettuce

2 cucumbers, peeled, seeded, and diced

1 large tomato, seeded and diced

½ cup shredded carrots

1 lemon, cut into wedges

1. Line a plate with parchment paper.

2. In a food processor, combine the chickpeas, parsley, tahini, garlic, flour, baking powder, and cumin. Season with salt and pepper and pulse until combined. Form the mixture into 8 balls and flatten each slightly. Place them on the prepared plate, cover it with plastic wrap, and freeze for 15 minutes.

3. Coat a skillet with cooking spray and set it over medium-high heat. Add the falafel and cook until lightly browned on all sides, about 5 minutes. Let the falafel cool.

4. Divide the lettuce among 4 serving bowls. Top each with the cucumbers, tomato, and shredded carrots. Place 2 falafel in each bowl and squeeze lemon juice over top.

MAKE AHEAD: Store the falafel in an airtight container in the refrigerator for up to 4 days.

Per serving: Calories: 216; Total fat: 7g; Carbohydrates: 34g; Fiber: 9g; Protein: 10g; Sodium: 362mg

Dilly Barley-Lentil Bowl with Feta and Mushrooms

Serves 5 / Prep time: 15 minutes / Cook time: 40 minutes

Chewy barley, meaty lentils, and earthy mushrooms go perfectly with sweet dill and salty feta. Add crunch with almonds and finish with a squeeze of fresh lemon juice.

1 cup pearl barley

Salt and black pepper

1 tablespoon olive oil

2 cups sliced button or cremini mushrooms

1 (15-ounce) can green lentils, drained and rinsed

¼ cup chopped fresh dill

½ cup crumbled feta cheese

¼ cup sliced almonds

1 lemon, cut into wedges

1. Fill a medium pot with water, add the barley, and season it with salt and pepper. Bring to a boil over medium-high heat. Lower the heat to low, cover, and cook until the barley is soft but still chewy, 25 to 30 minutes. Drain.

2. Meanwhile, in a skillet, warm the oil over medium-high heat. Add the mushrooms and sauté until the mushrooms have released most of their liquid, 8 to 10 minutes. Remove the skillet from the heat.

3. In a large bowl, mix together the barley, lentils, and dill and season with salt and pepper.

4. Divide the barley-lentil mixture among 5 serving bowls. Top with the mushrooms, feta, and almonds. Squeeze lemon juice over each bowl and serve.

MAKE AHEAD: Store the assembled bowls, covered, in the refrigerator for up to 4 days.

Per serving: Calories: 331; Total fat: 10g; Carbohydrates: 49g; Fiber: 12g; Protein: 15g; Sodium: 178mg

Millet and Black Bean Bowls

Serves 6 / Prep time: 15 minutes / Cook time: 35 minutes

Sweet potatoes pair perfectly with a garlic-lime sauce in this hearty dish. If you are looking to kick up the heat, add ¼ teaspoon ground chipotle chile to the sauce.

1 pound sweet potatoes, peeled and diced

2 red bell peppers, seeded and diced

1 tablespoon olive oil

1 teaspoon chili powder

Salt and black pepper

1 cup millet

2 cups water

1 avocado, pitted, peeled, and chopped

¼ cup plain yogurt

2 tablespoons freshly squeezed lime juice

1 teaspoon minced garlic

6 cups baby spinach

1 (15-ounce) can black beans, drained and rinsed

1. Preheat the oven to 375°F. Line a rimmed baking sheet with parchment paper.

2. In a large bowl, toss the sweet potatoes and bell peppers with the olive oil and chili powder. Season with salt and pepper. Spread out the vegetables in a single layer on the prepared baking sheet. Roast for 28 to 35 minutes, until tender.

3. Meanwhile, in a dry saucepan, toast the millet over medium heat, stirring, for 4 minutes. Add the water and season the millet with salt and pepper. Raise the heat to high and bring to a boil. Lower the heat to medium-low, cover, and simmer until the liquid is absorbed, about 15 minutes.

4. In a food processor, combine the avocado, yogurt, lime juice, and garlic, season the mixture with salt and pepper, and process until smooth.

5. Divide the spinach among 6 serving bowls and top each with the sweet potato mixture, millet, and black beans. Drizzle each bowl with the avocado sauce.

MAKE AHEAD: Store the bowls, covered, in the refrigerator for up to 2 days. Store the sauce separately and place plastic wrap directly on its surface to prevent browning.

Per serving: Calories: 346; Total fat: 8g; Carbohydrates: 60g; Fiber: 14g; Protein: 11g; Sodium: 88mg

Red Beans and Quinoa

Serves 6 / Prep time: 10 minutes / Cook time: 35 minutes

Red beans and rice is a classic Southern dish, and here I've upped the protein by swapping out the rice for quinoa. I'm glad I did because it tastes so good!

⅔ cup quinoa, rinsed

1 cup water

Salt and black pepper

1 tablespoon olive oil

1 onion, diced

1 red bell pepper, seeded and diced

3 celery stalks, thinly sliced

1 teaspoon smoked paprika

1 teaspoon liquid smoke

1 (15-ounce) can red kidney beans, drained and rinsed

¾ cup vegetable broth

1 tablespoon soy sauce

1. In a dry saucepan, toast the quinoa over medium heat for 4 minutes. Add the water, season the quinoa with salt and pepper, and bring to a simmer. Lower the heat to low and simmer until the liquid is absorbed, about 25 minutes. Remove the pan from the heat and let it sit, covered, for 5 minutes.

2. Meanwhile, in another saucepan, warm the olive oil over medium-high heat. Add the onion, bell pepper, celery, smoked paprika, and liquid smoke and sauté for 6 minutes. Season the veggies with salt and pepper. Add the beans, broth, and soy sauce and simmer until the mixture is thickened, about 20 minutes.

3. Divide the bean mixture among 6 serving bowls and top with the quinoa.

MAKE AHEAD: Store this dish in an airtight container in the refrigerator for up to 4 days.

Per serving: Calories: 180; Total fat: 4g; Carbohydrates: 30g; Fiber: 8g; Protein: 8g; Sodium: 247mg

Mexican-Inspired Quinoa Patties

Serves 6 / Prep time: 20 minutes / Cook time: 50 minutes

The trick to quinoa patties that don't fall apart is making sure a crust has formed before you try to flip them. Be patient: When they turn golden brown, they are ready to flip.

⅔ cup quinoa, rinsed

1 cup water

Salt and black pepper

1 cup canned black beans, drained and rinsed

4 large eggs, beaten

1 cup salsa

½ cup shredded cheddar cheese

1 cup bread crumbs

1 teaspoon minced garlic

1 teaspoon ground cumin

¼ teaspoon ground chipotle chile or cayenne pepper

2 tablespoons olive oil

1. In a dry saucepan, toast the quinoa over medium heat for 4 minutes. Add the water, season with salt and pepper, and bring to a boil. Lower the heat to low and simmer until the liquid is absorbed, about 25 minutes. Remove the pan from the heat and let it sit, covered, for 5 minutes.

2. In a large bowl, mix together the quinoa, black beans, eggs, salsa, cheese, bread crumbs, garlic, cumin, and ground chipotle. Season the mixture with salt and pepper and let it sit for 10 minutes.

3. Form the mixture into 6 patties.

4. In a skillet, warm the oil over medium-low heat. Add the patties to the skillet, being careful not to crowd the pan. Cover and cook until the patties are browned and their edges are dry, about 10 minutes. Flip the patties and cook until browned, another 8 to 10 minutes.

MAKE AHEAD: Store these quinoa patties in an airtight container in the refrigerator for up to 5 days or in the freezer for up to 3 months.

Per serving: Calories: 323; Total fat: 14g; Carbohydrates: 36g; Fiber: 6g; Protein: 15g; Sodium: 545mg

Garlicky Kale and White Beans

Serves 4 / Prep time: 10 minutes / Cook time: 7 minutes

Since kale is such a nutritional superstar, I try to work it into my diet as much as I can. Here I've paired it with wholesome white beans and a squeeze of fresh lemon juice.

2 tablespoons olive oil

2 teaspoons minced garlic

¼ teaspoon red pepper flakes

1 large bunch kale, stemmed and torn

Salt and black pepper

1 (15-ounce) can white beans, drained and rinsed

Grated zest and juice of 1 lemon

3 tablespoons toasted pine nuts

1. In a large skillet, warm the oil over medium heat. Add the garlic and red pepper flakes and sauté for 1 minute. Add the kale and season it with salt and pepper. Sauté until the kale is wilted, about 4 minutes.

2. Add the white beans and cook until heated through, about 2 more minutes. Add the lemon zest and juice, stir to combine, and top the dish with pine nuts.

MAKE AHEAD: Store this dish in an airtight container in the refrigerator for up to 4 days.

Per serving: Calories: 223; Total fat: 12g; Carbohydrates: 24g; Fiber: 10g; Protein: 8g; Sodium: 16mg

Spanish Brown Rice Burrito Bowls

Serves 6 / Prep time: 15 minutes / Cook time: 1 hour

Cook the rice on the weekend for a super-quick, flavor-packed meal throughout the week. Try adding corn and red bell pepper or whatever you have on hand.

1 tablespoon olive oil

1 onion, finely chopped

2 cups brown rice, rinsed

2½ cups vegetable broth

1 cup tomato puree

Salt and black pepper

½ cup sour cream or Greek yogurt

1 teaspoon minced garlic

Grated zest and juice of 1 lime

1 (15-ounce) can pinto beans, drained and rinsed

2 cups shredded sharp cheddar cheese

1 tomato, chopped

1 avocado, pitted, peeled, and sliced

1. In a large saucepan, warm the olive oil over medium-high heat. Add the onion and sauté for 8 minutes. Add the rice and sauté for 2 minutes. Add the vegetable broth and tomato puree, season the mixture with salt and pepper, and bring it to a boil.

2. Lower the heat to low, cover, and cook for 40 to 45 minutes, until tender. Remove the pan from the heat and let it sit, covered, for 10 minutes.

3. In a small bowl, mix together the sour cream, garlic, and lime zest and juice. Season the sauce with salt and pepper.

4. Divide the rice among 6 serving bowls. Top each bowl with pinto beans, cheese, tomato, and avocado. Drizzle each bowl with the lime sauce.

MAKE AHEAD: These bowls can be assembled without the avocado and sauce, covered, and stored in the refrigerator for up to 4 days. Slice the avocado just before serving.

Per serving: Calories: 535; Total fat: 24g; Carbohydrates: 69g; Fiber: 10g; Protein: 19g; Sodium: 610mg

Baked Butternut Squash Risotto

Serves 6 / Prep time: 15 minutes / Cook time: 45 minutes

Risotto without all the work? Count me in! Save prep time by using diced butternut squash found in the produce department of your grocery store.

3 tablespoons olive oil

1 onion, diced

1 teaspoon minced garlic

2 cups Arborio rice

1 cup dry white wine

4 cups diced
butternut squash

4½ cups vegetable broth

Salt and black pepper

2 tablespoons chopped
fresh sage

¾ cup grated vegetarian
Parmesan cheese

1. Preheat the oven to 375°F.

2. In a large Dutch oven, warm the olive oil over medium-high heat. Add the onion and sauté for 6 minutes. Add the garlic and sauté for 1 minute longer. Add the rice and sauté for 3 minutes. Add the wine and cook until it has mostly evaporated, about 3 more minutes.

3. Add the butternut squash and broth and bring the mixture to a boil. Season with salt and pepper. Cover the Dutch oven and carefully transfer it to the oven. Bake for 25 to 30 minutes.

4. Stir in the sage and Parmesan and let the dish sit, covered, for 5 to 10 minutes, then fluff with a fork.

MAKE AHEAD: Store this risotto in an airtight container in the refrigerator for up to 4 days.

Per serving: Calories: 447; Total fat: 12g; Carbohydrates: 75g; Fiber: 7g; Protein: 7g; Sodium: 764mg

Italian Farro Cakes

Serves 6 / Prep time: 15 minutes / Cook time: 35 minutes

Farro is an earthy, slightly sweet whole grain with an addictively chewy texture. Look for pearled farro, which cooks much faster than semi-pearled or whole-grain farro.

1 cup pearled farro

2 cups water

Salt and black pepper

2 cups shredded kale

1 cup shredded mozzarella cheese

¼ cup chopped sun-dried tomatoes

1 teaspoon Italian seasoning

1 cup bread crumbs

2 tablespoons all-purpose flour

4 large eggs, beaten

2 tablespoons avocado oil

1. In a medium saucepan, combine the farro and water and bring them to a boil over high heat. Season with salt and pepper. Lower the heat to medium, cover, and simmer until the grains are tender, about 20 minutes. Drain.

2. Transfer the farro to a large bowl and add the kale, mozzarella, sun-dried tomatoes, and Italian seasoning. Season the mixture with salt and pepper. Add the bread crumbs and flour and toss well. Add the eggs, mix well, and let the mixture sit for 5 minutes.

3. Using a ¼-cup measure, form the mixture into 6 patties.

4. In a large skillet, warm the oil over medium heat. Add the patties, cover, and cook until browned, 3 to 4 minutes. Flip the patties and cook, covered, until browned on the other side, 3 to 4 more minutes.

MAKE AHEAD: Store these patties in an airtight container in the refrigerator for up to 4 days or in the freezer for up to 3 months.

Per serving: Calories: 348; Total fat: 15g; Carbohydrates: 40g; Fiber: 5g; Protein: 16g; Sodium: 341mg

Parmesan Polenta with Garlic Roasted Broccoli

Serves 6 / Prep time: 10 minutes / Cook time: 30 minutes

Polenta is often overlooked as a base for grain bowls, but its delicious flavor and creamy texture make it a welcome change.

8 cups water

⅛ teaspoon baking soda

Salt and black pepper

2 cups polenta

2 cups grated vegetarian Parmesan cheese

3 tablespoons unsalted butter

1 pound broccoli florets

1 tablespoon olive oil

1 teaspoon minced garlic

¼ cup pine nuts, toasted

1. Preheat the oven to 425°F. Line a rimmed baking sheet with parchment paper.

2. In a large pot, combine the water and baking soda and bring to a boil over high heat. Season the water with salt and pepper, stir in the polenta, and return the mixture to a boil. Lower the heat to low, cover, and cook for 4 minutes. Stir, cover again, and cook for 25 minutes. Stir in the Parmesan and butter.

3. Meanwhile, toss the broccoli with the olive oil and garlic and spread it out in a single layer on the prepared baking sheet. Season the broccoli with salt and pepper and roast for 25 minutes.

4. Divide the polenta among 6 serving bowls and top each bowl with broccoli. Sprinkle each bowl with the pine nuts.

MAKE AHEAD: Store this dish in an airtight container in the refrigerator for up to 2 days. Reheat over medium-low heat, adding water ¼ cup at a time as needed.

Per serving: Calories: 382; Total fat: 17g; Carbohydrates: 49g; Fiber: 5g; Protein: 7g; Sodium: 422mg

Ultimate Paella

Serves 6 / Prep time: 15 minutes / Cook time: 31 minutes

I often double this recipe and use the leftovers to make stuffed peppers the next day: Stuff bell peppers with the rice and bake at 425°F for 20 to 30 minutes, until the peppers start to blister.

1 tablespoon olive oil

1 onion, diced

2 red bell peppers, seeded and sliced

1 teaspoon minced garlic

1½ teaspoons smoked paprika

Salt and black pepper

2¼ cups vegetable broth

1 (8-ounce) package yellow rice, such as Zatarain's

1½ cups frozen baby peas, thawed

1 (14-ounce) can artichoke hearts, drained and chopped

⅓ cup green olives, pitted and chopped

2 tablespoons freshly squeezed lemon juice

1. In a large skillet, warm the olive oil over medium-high heat. Add the onion, bell peppers, garlic, and smoked paprika. Season the veggies with salt and pepper and sauté for 8 minutes.

2. Add the broth and yellow rice and bring to a boil. Lower the heat to medium-low, cover, and simmer for 18 minutes.

3. Add the peas, artichoke hearts, and green olives and stir to combine. Cook, without stirring, until the rice is al dente and forms a crust at the bottom of the pan, about 5 more minutes. Stir in the lemon juice and serve.

MAKE AHEAD: Store this paella in an airtight container in the refrigerator for up to 4 days.

Per serving: Calories: 236; Total fat: 4g; Carbohydrates: 43g; Fiber: 7g; Protein: 8g; Sodium: 833mg

Mushroom Farro Risotto

Serves 6 / Prep time: 10 minutes / Cook time: 50 minutes

I have always had a soft spot for risotto, and in this version, the nutty Parmesan and creamy goat cheese balance perfectly with earthy mushrooms and chewy farro. Prepare for clean plates all around.

2 tablespoons
unsalted butter

1 onion, diced

1 pound cremini
mushrooms, sliced

Salt and black pepper

2 cups pearled farro

¾ cup dry white wine

4 cups vegetable
broth, divided

¾ cup grated vegetarian
Parmesan cheese

2 ounces crumbled
goat cheese

2 tablespoons chopped
fresh parsley

1. In a Dutch oven, melt the butter over medium-high heat. Add the onion and mushrooms, season them with salt and pepper, and sauté for 6 minutes. Add the farro and sauté for 4 more minutes.

2. Add the wine and cook for 1½ minutes. Add 2 cups broth and bring the mixture to a boil. Lower the heat to medium and simmer, adding the remaining broth ½ cup at a time and stirring frequently, until the liquid is absorbed, 25 to 35 minutes.

3. Stir in the Parmesan and goat cheese. Remove the pot from the heat, cover it, and let it sit for 5 minutes. Stir the risotto and sprinkle it with the parsley.

MAKE AHEAD: This risotto is best fresh, but you can make it up to 1 day ahead and store it in an airtight container in the refrigerator.

Per serving: Calories: 281; Total fat: 11g; Carbohydrates: 34g; Fiber: 4g; Protein: 9g; Sodium: 778mg

Bulgur Taco Salad

Serves 4 / Prep time: 15 minutes / Cook time: 15 minutes

I like to use quick-cooking bulgur, which takes just 10 minutes to prepare. Check the label of your brand and adjust the cooking time if needed. If you eat gluten-free, quinoa makes a great substitute.

1 canned chipotle chile plus 1 tablespoon adobo sauce

4 garlic cloves, minced

3 tablespoons freshly squeezed lime juice

2 tablespoons soy sauce

2 tablespoons olive oil

2 tablespoons taco seasoning

2 cups water

1 cup quick-cooking bulgur

6 cups chopped romaine lettuce

1 cup frozen corn, thawed

½ cup shredded cheddar cheese

1 avocado, pitted, peeled, and diced

1½ cups salsa

1. In a blender or food processor, combine the chipotle and adobo sauce, garlic, lime juice, soy sauce, olive oil, taco seasoning, and water and process until smooth.

2. In a large pot, toast the bulgur for 1 minute over medium-high heat. Add the chipotle mixture and bring it to a boil. Lower the heat to low, cover, and simmer for 10 minutes. Remove the pot from the heat and let it sit, covered, for 10 minutes.

3. Divide the lettuce among 4 serving bowls. Top each bowl with bulgur, corn, cheddar cheese, and avocado. Drizzle each bowl with the salsa and serve.

MAKE AHEAD: Store the bulgur in an airtight container in the refrigerator for up to 4 days.

Per serving: Calories: 393; Total fat: 18g; Carbohydrates: 53g; Fiber: 12g; Protein: 13g; Sodium: 1584mg

Cranberry-Apple Wild Rice Pilaf

Serves 6 / Prep time: 15 minutes / Cook time: 59 minutes

This aromatic pilaf reminds me of fall and makes a great addition to any holiday table. The cooking time for wild rice can vary by brand, so check the package and adjust accordingly.

2 tablespoons olive oil

1 onion, chopped

1 tablespoon minced garlic

2 cups wild rice

4½ cups vegetable broth

1 teaspoon dried thyme

Salt and black pepper

1 green apple, cored and diced

1 tablespoon freshly squeezed lemon juice

1 cup dried cranberries

½ cup chopped pecans

1. In a large saucepan, warm the olive oil over medium-high heat. Add the onion and sauté for 6 minutes. Add the garlic and sauté for 1 minute longer. Add the wild rice and sauté for 2 minutes. Add the broth and thyme, season the mixture with salt and pepper, and bring it to a boil.

2. Lower the heat to medium-low, cover the pan, and simmer until tender, 35 to 40 minutes. Remove the pan from the heat and let it sit, covered, for 10 minutes.

3. In a small bowl, mix together the diced apple and lemon juice. Add the apple, dried cranberries, and pecans to the rice and stir until combined.

MAKE AHEAD: Store this pilaf in an airtight container in the refrigerator for up to 1 day. To store for up to 4 days, don't add the apple until just before serving.

Per serving: Calories: 424; Total fat: 11g; Carbohydrates: 77g; Fiber: 7g; Protein: 11g; Sodium: 494mg

Mediterranean Grain Bowls

Serves 4 / Prep time: 10 minutes

Say goodbye to lunchtime boredom. This recipe is highly adaptable—use any grain you like and add artichokes, sun-dried tomatoes, roasted eggplant, or whatever else strikes your fancy. Tzatziki (see Roasted Chickpea Gyros, page 95) would make a great swap for the hummus.

4 cups cooked grains, such as quinoa, brown rice, or millet

1 cup quartered grape tomatoes

2 cups chopped spinach

1 (15-ounce) can chickpeas, drained and rinsed

¾ cup sliced pepperoncini, drained

½ cup crumbled feta cheese

⅓ cup pitted sliced kalamata olives

2 tablespoons freshly squeezed lemon juice

½ cup hummus

Salt and black pepper

1. Divide the grains among 4 serving bowls. Add one-quarter of the tomatoes, spinach, chickpeas, pepperoncini, feta, and olives to each bowl.

2. Drizzle the lemon juice over the bowls and top each with the hummus. Season the bowls with salt and pepper.

MAKE AHEAD: These bowls can be stored, covered, in the refrigerator for up to 3 days.

Per serving: Calories: 419; Total fat: 13g; Carbohydrates: 61g; Fiber: 14g; Protein: 17g; Sodium: 1218mg

Couscous-Stuffed Tomatoes

Serves 6 / Prep time: 15 minutes / Cook time: 25 minutes

Salty feta and briny olives will keep you coming back for this perfect light dinner, particularly during summer when tomatoes are at their peak.

6 medium tomatoes, halved lengthwise

Salt and black pepper

½ cup vegetable broth

1 teaspoon olive oil

⅓ cup couscous

¼ cup chopped pitted olives

¼ cup crumbled feta cheese

2 tablespoons chopped fresh parsley

3 tablespoons grated vegetarian Parmesan cheese

1. Preheat the oven to 425°F. Line a rimmed baking sheet with parchment paper.

2. Spoon the pulp out of the centers of the tomatoes (reserve for another use), sprinkle them with salt, and place them, cut-sides down, on a paper towel to drain for 5 minutes.

3. Meanwhile, in a small saucepan, combine the broth and olive oil, season them with salt and pepper, and bring to a boil over medium-high heat. Add the couscous, cover, and remove the pan from the heat. Let it sit for 5 minutes, then fluff the couscous with a fork.

4. Place the tomatoes, cut-sides up, on the prepared baking sheet and bake for 7 minutes. Let them cool slightly. Lower the oven temperature to 350°F.

5. Add the olives, feta, and parsley to the couscous and stir to combine. Stuff the mixture into the tomato halves, sprinkle them with the Parmesan, and bake until the cheese is lightly browned, 10 to 12 minutes.

MAKE AHEAD: Store the couscous filling in an airtight container in the refrigerator for up to 4 days.

Per serving: Calories: 97; Total fat: 4g; Carbohydrates: 14g; Fiber: 2g; Protein: 3g; Sodium: 210mg

Turmeric Couscous with Apricots and Pistachios

Serves 6 / Prep time: 10 minutes / Cook time: 5 minutes

This versatile dish is pretty enough for your holiday table and equally suited to eating straight from the fridge on busy mornings. Add a squeeze of lemon juice to lift up leftovers.

2 cups vegetable broth

1 tablespoon olive oil

Salt and black pepper

1½ cups couscous

⅓ cup chopped dried apricots

1 teaspoon ground turmeric

1 tablespoon freshly squeezed lemon juice

⅓ cup pistachios

1. In a medium saucepan, combine the broth and olive oil, season them with salt and pepper, and bring the mixture to a boil over medium-high heat. Stir in the couscous, apricots, and turmeric. Remove the pan from the heat, cover it, and let it sit for 5 minutes.

2. Fluff the couscous with a fork, then stir in the lemon juice and top the couscous with the pistachios.

MAKE AHEAD: Store this dish in an airtight container in the refrigerator for up to 4 days.

Per serving: Calories: 244; Total fat: 6g; Carbohydrates: 41g; Fiber: 4g; Protein: 7g; Sodium: 223mg

Broccoli Rice Bake

Serves 6 / Prep time: 20 minutes / Cook time: 1 hour

This easy-to-throw-together casserole is a vegetarian version of one I grew up eating. Try different cheeses, whatever you have on hand. Goat cheese is my particular favorite.

2 cups water

1 cup long-grain white rice

Salt and black pepper

3 tablespoons unsalted butter

3 tablespoons all-purpose flour

1¼ cups milk

1½ cups shredded cheddar cheese, divided

1 teaspoon garlic powder

5 ounces frozen broccoli, thawed and drained

⅓ cup panko bread crumbs

1. Preheat the oven to 350°F. Coat a 1-quart baking dish with cooking spray.

2. In a saucepan, bring the water to a boil over medium-high heat. Add the rice, season it with salt and pepper, and bring it back to a boil.

3. Lower the heat to low, cover, and cook for 18 minutes. Remove the pan from the heat and let it sit, covered, for 10 minutes.

4. In another saucepan, melt the butter over medium heat. Add the flour and cook, whisking constantly, for 2 minutes. Add the milk and cook, stirring, until it thickens, about 5 minutes.

5. Lower the heat to low, add 1 cup cheese and the garlic powder, season the mixture with salt and pepper, and stir until the cheese melts.

6. Remove the pan from the heat. Add the rice and broccoli and stir to combine. Transfer the mixture to the baking dish and top it with the remaining ½ cup cheese and the bread crumbs.

7. Bake for 30 minutes. Let sit for 5 to 10 minutes before serving.

MAKE AHEAD: Store the baked casserole, covered, in the refrigerator for up to 4 days.

Per serving: Calories: 350; Total fat: 17g; Carbohydrates: 37g; Fiber: 2g; Protein: 13g; Sodium: 261mg

Anytime Eggs

Chive and Ricotta Scrambled Eggs

Serves 4 / Prep time: 5 minutes / Cook time: 5 minutes

I had never been the biggest fan of scrambled eggs by themselves, but this recipe changed that. In this jazzed-up version, fluffy, creamy eggs are brightened with a touch of fresh chives.

8 large eggs

2 tablespoons milk

Salt and black pepper

2 tablespoons unsalted butter

½ cup ricotta cheese

¼ cup chopped fresh chives

1. In a medium bowl, whisk the eggs and milk until frothy, about 1 minute. (If you have the time, let them sit at room temperature for 15 minutes.) Season the egg mixture with salt and pepper.

2. In a large skillet, melt the butter over medium-high heat. Whisk the egg mixture briefly and add it to the skillet. Cook, scraping the bottoms and sides of the pan with a spatula, until the eggs start to solidify.

3. Add the ricotta and continue to cook, stirring constantly, until the eggs hold their shape and no liquid egg remains. Stir in the chives and serve immediately.

SUBSTITUTE: If you don't have chives on hand, chopped fresh parsley works well, too.

Per serving: Calories: 258; Total fat: 20g; Carbohydrates: 4g; Fiber: <1g; Protein: 15g; Sodium: 162mg

Egg in a Hole

Serves 4 / Prep time: 10 minutes / Cook time: 15 minutes

This kid-friendly breakfast classic never gets old. I like to use a country-style white bread from the bakery, but any bread will do. A sprinkling of fresh parsley or chives is a nice way to finish this dish.

4 tablespoons unsalted butter

4 slices bread

4 large eggs

Salt and black pepper

½ cup shredded cheddar cheese

¼ teaspoon red pepper flakes

1. Line a rimmed baking sheet with parchment paper and spray it with cooking spray. Place it in the oven and preheat the oven to 425°F.

2. Spread the butter on both sides of each slice of bread. Using a 2½-inch cookie cutter, cut holes from the center of each slice. Place the bread and holes on the prepared baking sheet and bake for 5 minutes.

3. Remove the baking sheet from the oven and crack 1 egg into each hole in the bread. Season each egg with salt and pepper. Sprinkle the cheese on top.

4. Bake for 6 to 10 minutes, until the whites are set but the yolks are still runny. Sprinkle each egg with red pepper flakes.

SUBSTITUTE: Feel free to use whatever cheese you like here. Make this gluten-free by using gluten-free bread.

Per serving: Calories: 337; Total fat: 22g; Carbohydrates: 22g; Fiber: 1g; Protein: 13g; Sodium: 442mg

Savory Oat Bowl with Fried Eggs

Serves 4 / Prep time: 10 minutes / Cook time: 15 minutes

Oats have long been a favorite of mine, but lately I've bucked tradition and opted for savory oats rather than sweet, making this bowl just as good for lunch as it is for breakfast.

½ cup minced red onion

2 cups old-fashioned oats

3½ cups vegetable broth

¼ cup nutritional yeast (optional)

1 teaspoon liquid smoke

Salt and black pepper

1 tablespoon olive oil

4 large eggs

¾ cup halved grape tomatoes

1 avocado, pitted, peeled, and sliced

1. Coat a saucepan with cooking spray and set it over medium heat. Add the onion and sauté for 5 minutes. Add the oats, broth, nutritional yeast (if using), and liquid smoke. Season the mixture with salt and pepper and cook, stirring, to your desired doneness, about 5 minutes.

2. In a large skillet, warm the olive oil over medium heat. Crack the eggs into the pan and cook them to your desired doneness, 1 to 3 minutes.

3. Divide the oatmeal among 4 serving bowls. Top each bowl with an egg and one-quarter of the tomato and avocado.

MAKE AHEAD: Store this oatmeal in an airtight container in the refrigerator for up to 3 days.

Per serving: Calories: 390; Total fat: 23g; Carbohydrates: 36g; Fiber: 7g; Protein: 12g; Sodium: 633mg

Breakfast Quesadillas with Spinach and Red Pepper

Serves 4 / Prep time: 10 minutes / Cook time: 25 minutes

I never considered quesadillas breakfast food, but that changed one day when the fridge and pantry were dreadfully bare and I came up with an easy meal to fuel a family outing.

1 cup chopped spinach

½ red bell pepper, seeded and chopped

4 large eggs

¼ cup milk

Salt and black pepper

½ cup grated cheddar cheese

4 large flour tortillas

¼ cup guacamole

¼ cup salsa

1. Coat a skillet with cooking spray and set it over medium heat. Add the spinach and bell pepper and sauté for 4 minutes.

2. In a medium bowl, beat together the eggs and milk. Season the mixture with salt and pepper.

3. Add the egg mixture to the pan and cook, stirring often, until the eggs are cooked through. Transfer the eggs and veggies to a plate.

4. Wipe out the pan with a paper towel and coat it again with cooking spray; set it over medium heat. Place 1 tortilla in the skillet. Spread one-fourth of the egg mixture on the tortilla. Top it with one-fourth of the cheese, then fold the tortilla in half. Cook until golden brown, 3 to 5 minutes per side. Repeat with the rest of the tortillas, eggs, and cheese. Serve with the guacamole and salsa.

MAKE AHEAD: Store the sautéed vegetables in an airtight container in the refrigerator for up to 4 days.

Per serving: Calories: 322; Total fat: 18g; Carbohydrates: 35g; Fiber: 4g; Protein: 15g; Sodium: 670mg

Sheet Pan Breakfast Sandwiches

Serves 4 / Prep time: 10 minutes / Cook time: 10 minutes

This is one of my absolute favorite ways to power my morning. You can buy egg rings at most kitchen stores—or use round metal cookie cutters in a pinch.

4 large eggs

2 tablespoons milk

Salt and black pepper

4 tablespoons unsalted butter

4 English muffins, split

4 slices cheddar cheese

1 cup chopped spinach

4 slices tomato

4 teaspoons sriracha

1. Line a rimmed baking sheet with parchment paper and place it in the oven. Preheat the oven to 350°F. Coat 4 (3½-inch) egg rings with cooking spray.

2. In a bowl, whisk together the eggs and milk. Season the mixture with salt and pepper. Spread the butter on the English muffin halves.

3. Remove the baking sheet from the oven and place the egg rings on it. Divide the egg mixture among the egg rings. Place the English muffins on the baking sheet, buttered-sides up. Bake for 8 minutes.

4. Place the cheese slices on the English muffin tops and bake for 2 more minutes, until the cheese is melted.

5. Carefully remove the eggs from the egg rings and place them on the English muffin bottoms. Top each egg with some spinach and a tomato slice. Drizzle each sandwich with sriracha. Cover the sandwiches with the English muffin tops.

MAKE AHEAD: Store these sandwiches, covered tightly with plastic wrap, in the refrigerator for up to 1 day.

Per serving: Calories: 426; Total fat: 27g; Carbohydrates: 29g; Fiber: 2g; Protein: 18g; Sodium: 708mg

Poached Eggs with Roasted Vegetables

Serves 4 / Prep time: 10 minutes / Cook time: 15 minutes

This recipe is easy enough to make for yourself, but special enough for company. A sprinkle of fresh dill and crumbled goat cheese is an excellent way to finish it.

1 pound asparagus, trimmed

8 ounces radishes, trimmed and halved

1 tablespoon olive oil

1 teaspoon garlic powder

Salt and black pepper

1 tablespoon vinegar

4 large eggs

1. Preheat the oven to 425°F. Line a rimmed baking sheet with parchment paper.

2. In a large bowl, toss the asparagus and radishes with the olive oil and garlic powder. Season them with salt and pepper. Spread the veggies out in a single layer on the prepared baking sheet. Roast them for 10 to 12 minutes, until the asparagus is crisp-tender.

3. Bring a medium pot of water to a boil over high heat. Lower the heat to medium and add the vinegar. Crack 1 egg into a small bowl or ramekin. Gently slip the egg into the water; repeat with the remaining eggs. Cook the eggs until the whites are set but the yolks are still runny, about 3 minutes.

4. Divide the vegetables among 4 plates and top each plate with a poached egg.

MAKE AHEAD: Store the roasted vegetables in an airtight container in the refrigerator for up to 1 day.

Per serving: Calories: 142; Total fat: 9g; Carbohydrates: 8g; Fiber: 3g; Protein: 9g; Sodium: 87mg

Sweet Potato Hash with Eggs

Serves 6 / Prep time: 15 minutes / Cook time: 20 minutes

This hearty breakfast is perfect for weekend mornings. A food processor with a shredding disk makes quick work of grating the sweet potatoes or, if you'd prefer, you can spiralize them.

2 tablespoons olive oil

3 large sweet potatoes, peeled and grated

1 red bell pepper, seeded and diced

1 teaspoon smoked paprika

1 teaspoon garlic powder

Salt and black pepper

6 large eggs

1. Preheat the oven to 400°F.

2. In a large oven-safe skillet, warm the olive oil over medium-high heat. Add the sweet potatoes, bell pepper, smoked paprika, and garlic powder. Season the hash with salt and pepper and sauté for 10 minutes. Remove the skillet from the heat.

3. Using a spoon, make 6 indentations in the sweet potato hash to accommodate the eggs. Crack 1 egg into a small bowl or ramekin and carefully slip it into one of the spaces; repeat with the remaining eggs. Season the eggs with salt and pepper.

4. Transfer the skillet to the oven and bake until the egg whites are set but the yolks are still runny, 7 to 10 minutes.

MAKE AHEAD: Store the sweet potato hash in an airtight container in the refrigerator for up to 2 days.

Per serving: Calories: 213; Total fat: 10g; Carbohydrates: 23g; Fiber: 4g; Protein: 8g; Sodium: 120mg

Chiles Rellenos Breakfast Casserole

Serves 4 / Prep time: 10 minutes / Cook time: 30 minutes

This Tex-Mex casserole is a fun way to mix up your morning routine. I like to cut it into individual servings and freeze them for up to 3 months, then defrost and reheat them for quick morning meals.

8 large eggs

1 cup milk

2 tablespoons all-purpose flour

1 teaspoon garlic powder

Salt and black pepper

1½ cups grated cheddar cheese, divided

1 (8-ounce) can diced green chiles, drained

1 tablespoon hot sauce

1. Preheat the oven to 350°F. Coat an 8-inch square baking dish with cooking spray.

2. In a large bowl, whisk together the eggs, milk, flour, and garlic powder. Season the mixture with salt and pepper. Add 1 cup cheese, the green chiles, and hot sauce and stir to combine. Transfer the mixture to the prepared baking dish and top it with the remaining ½ cup cheese.

3. Bake for 30 minutes, or until the eggs are set.

MAKE AHEAD: Store this casserole in an airtight container in the refrigerator for up to 4 days.

Per serving: Calories: 377; Total fat: 26g; Carbohydrates: 13g; Fiber: 2g; Protein: 23g; Sodium: 695mg

Fried Egg Breakfast Salad

Serves 4 / Prep time: 10 minutes / Cook time: 3 minutes

While salads for breakfast are officially a thing these days, I was eating them long before they were cool. It is the best way I know to pave the way for a healthy day.

⅓ cup plus 1 tablespoon olive oil

2 tablespoons rice vinegar

1 tablespoon freshly squeezed lemon juice

Salt and black pepper

4 large eggs

6 cups mixed greens

½ cup halved grape tomatoes

½ recipe Vegetarian Bacon (page 22)

1. In a small bowl, whisk together ⅓ cup olive oil, the rice vinegar, and lemon juice. Season the mixture with salt and pepper.

2. In a large skillet, warm the remaining 1 tablespoon olive oil over medium heat. Crack the eggs into the pan and cook them to your desired doneness, 1 to 3 minutes.

3. In a large bowl, combine the greens, tomatoes, and bacon. Add the dressing and toss to combine. Divide the salad among 4 plates and top each salad with an egg.

MAKE AHEAD: Store the dressing in an airtight container in the refrigerator for up to 4 days.

Per serving: Calories: 351; Total fat: 32g; Carbohydrates: 9g; Fiber: 4g; Protein: 8g; Sodium: 154mg

Chilaquiles

Serves 4 / Prep time: 10 minutes / Cook time: 25 minutes

Chilaquiles are like breakfast nachos, and I'm not sure there is a better way to start the day. Serve them with a dollop of sour cream, a squeeze of lime, and fresh cilantro.

4 tablespoons olive oil, divided

8 corn tortillas, quartered

1 large onion, chopped

1 teaspoon minced garlic

1 (16-ounce) jar salsa

1 (15-ounce) can pinto beans, drained and rinsed

Salt and black pepper

4 large eggs

¾ cup shredded Mexican-style cheese blend

1. In a large skillet, warm 3 tablespoons oil over medium-high heat. Add half of the tortilla pieces and cook for 1 to 2 minutes. Flip the pieces and cook until golden, 1 to 2 minutes more. Transfer the pieces to paper towels to drain and repeat with the remaining tortillas.

2. Add the onion to the skillet and sauté for 6 minutes. Add the garlic and sauté for 1 minute longer. Stir in the salsa and beans and cook until warmed through, about 5 minutes. Season the mixture with salt and pepper.

3. In another large skillet, heat the remaining 1 tablespoon oil over medium heat. Crack the eggs into the pan and cook them to your desired doneness, 1 to 3 minutes.

4. Stir the tortillas into the bean mixture and divide the beans and tortillas among 4 serving plates. Sprinkle each bowl with cheese and top each plate with a fried egg.

MAKE AHEAD: Store the bean mixture in an airtight container in the refrigerator for up to 3 days.

Per serving: Calories: 517; Total fat: 27g; Carbohydrates: 50g; Fiber: 6g; Protein: 21g; Sodium: 1298mg

Zucchini Frittata

Serves 4 / Prep time: 10 minutes / Cook time: 15 minutes

Looking to clean out the cheese and crisper drawers in your fridge? This is your solution. You can substitute whatever produce and cheese you have on hand.

8 large eggs

¼ cup milk

1 teaspoon sriracha

1 teaspoon chili powder

1 teaspoon smoked paprika

Salt and black pepper

1 large zucchini, diced

1 bunch scallions, thinly sliced

1 jalapeño, seeded and diced

1 cup shredded cheddar cheese

1. Position an oven rack in the upper third of the oven and preheat the broiler.

2. In a large bowl, whisk together the eggs, milk, sriracha, chili powder, and smoked paprika. Season the mixture with salt and pepper.

3. Coat a large oven-safe skillet with cooking spray and set it over medium heat. Add the zucchini, scallions, and jalapeño and sauté until softened, 3 to 5 minutes. Sprinkle the cheese over the vegetables.

4. Pour the egg mixture over the veggies and cheese and cook until the eggs are partially set, lifting the eggs to allow uncooked portions to flow underneath, 5 to 6 minutes.

5. Transfer the skillet to the oven and broil until the frittata is browned, 2 to 3 minutes. Run a spatula around the edge of the pan to loosen the frittata, then cut it into wedges.

MAKE AHEAD: Store this frittata in an airtight container in the refrigerator for up to 3 days. Reheat in a 350°F oven. You can also serve it cold for a quick weekday-morning breakfast.

Per serving: Calories: 306; Total fat: 21g; Carbohydrates: 8g; Fiber: 2g; Protein: 21g; Sodium: 380mg

Broccoli and Goat Cheese Quiche

Serves 8 / Prep time: 15 minutes / Cook time: 1 hour 30 minutes

Quiche is a brunch classic that works just as well for a Sunday night dinner. Freeze leftovers (if you have any) for up to 3 months.

1 (9-inch) piecrust, thawed if frozen

3 large eggs

1 cup milk or half-and-half

¼ teaspoon cayenne pepper

Salt and black pepper

1 onion, diced

2 cups finely chopped broccoli

4 ounces goat cheese, crumbled

1. Place a rimmed baking sheet in the oven and preheat the oven to 350°F.

2. Roll out the piecrust and place it on a 9-inch pie plate. Cover the dough with parchment paper and add dried beans or pie weights. Bake for 20 minutes. Remove the beans/weights and the parchment and bake for 10 minutes more.

3. In a large bowl, whisk together the eggs, milk, and cayenne. Season the mixture with salt and pepper.

4. Coat a large skillet with cooking spray and set it over medium heat. Add the onion and broccoli and sauté until tender, about 8 minutes. Let the vegetables cool slightly.

5. Sprinkle half of the goat cheese over the crust. Top it with the vegetables, then the remaining goat cheese. Pour the egg mixture over the vegetables and cheese.

6. Place the quiche on the hot baking sheet and bake 40 to 50 minutes, until set. Let the quiche sit for 10 minutes before cutting it into wedges.

MAKE AHEAD: Store this quiche, tightly covered with plastic wrap, in the refrigerator for up to 3 days.

Per serving: Calories: 211; Total fat: 13g; Carbohydrates: 15g; Fiber: 1g; Protein: 9g; Sodium: 189mg

Spanish Tortilla

Serves 6 / Prep time: 20 minutes / Cook time: 1 hour 10 minutes

A Spanish tortilla is like an omelet or frittata with potatoes—perfect for when you need a hearty breakfast that will keep you fueled all morning.

6 tablespoons olive oil, divided

1 onion, diced

Salt and black pepper

1 teaspoon minced garlic

1¼ pounds russet potatoes, peeled and thinly sliced

8 large eggs

2 tablespoons milk

¼ cup shredded Manchego cheese

1. Preheat the oven to 375°F.

2. In a large oven-safe skillet, warm 1 tablespoon olive oil over medium heat. Add the onion, season it with salt and pepper, and sauté for 8 minutes. Add the garlic and sauté for 1 minute. Transfer to a plate.

3. Add 4 tablespoons oil to the skillet. Working in batches, sauté the potatoes, 8 to 10 minutes.

4. In a large bowl, whisk together the eggs and milk. Season with salt and pepper. Stir in the potatoes.

5. Wipe out the skillet and set it over medium-high heat, and warm the remaining 1 tablespoon olive oil. Add the potato and egg mixture and spread it out in the skillet. Cook without disturbing for 1 minute. Cook over low heat until the edges are set, about 8 minutes.

6. Transfer the skillet to the oven and bake until the potatoes are tender and the eggs are set, 15 to 20 minutes. Sprinkle with the cheese and bake until melted, about 5 minutes. Cut into wedges and serve.

MAKE AHEAD: Store this tortilla, tightly covered with plastic wrap, in the refrigerator for up to 4 days.

Per serving: Calories: 318; Total fat: 22g; Carbohydrates: 20g; Fiber: 2g; Protein: 11g; Sodium: 121mg

Egg Salad

Serves 6 / Prep time: 15 minutes / Cook time: 5 minutes

Serve this salad on its own or use it to make a sandwich. To lighten it up, substitute plain Greek yogurt for half of the mayonnaise.

12 large eggs

½ cup mayonnaise

2 teaspoons Dijon mustard

1 tablespoon chopped fresh dill

1 tablespoon chopped fresh chives

1 teaspoon smoked paprika

Salt and black pepper

1. Place the eggs in a large saucepan and cover them with water by 1 inch. Set the pan over high heat, bring to a boil, and cook for 1 minute. Cover the pan, remove it from the heat, and let it sit for 10 minutes.

2. Fill a large bowl with ice cubes and water. Drain the eggs and transfer them to the ice-water bath to cool.

3. Peel the eggs, chop them, and transfer them to a large bowl.

4. In a small bowl, mix together the mayonnaise, Dijon mustard, dill, chives, and paprika. Season the mixture with salt and pepper.

5. Add the mayonnaise mixture to the eggs and stir to combine.

MAKE AHEAD: Store this egg salad in an airtight container in the refrigerator for up to 4 days.

Per serving: Calories: 283; Total fat: 25g; Carbohydrates: 2g; Fiber: <1g; Protein: 13g; Sodium: 281mg

Green Shakshuka

Serves 6 / Prep time: 15 minutes / Cook time: 25 minutes

Traditional shakshuka calls for eggs in tomato sauce, but this greened-up version is every bit as enticing. Enjoy it for breakfast or serve it with White Bean Salad with Tahini Dressing (page 105) for dinner.

1 tablespoon olive oil

1 onion, chopped

12 cups chopped kale

2 teaspoons minced garlic

Salt and black pepper

6 large eggs

½ cup crumbled goat cheese

1 avocado, pitted, peeled, and sliced

1 jalapeño, seeded and sliced

1. Preheat the oven to 375°F.

2. In a large oven-safe skillet or Dutch oven, warm the oil over medium-high heat. Add the onion and sauté for 5 minutes. Add the kale in batches and sauté until it is wilted, 3 to 4 minutes. Add the garlic and season the kale mixture with salt and pepper.

3. Using a spoon, make 6 wells in the greens. Crack 1 egg into a small bowl or ramekin and carefully slip it into one of the wells; repeat with the remaining eggs. Scatter the goat cheese over the mixture.

4. Transfer the skillet to the oven and bake until the egg whites are set but the yolks are a bit runny, 10 to 15 minutes.

5. Top the shakshuka with the avocado and jalapeño slices.

MAKE AHEAD: Store the sautéed onion and kale in an airtight container in the refrigerator for up to 4 days.

Per serving: Calories: 202; Total fat: 15g; Carbohydrates: 7g; Fiber: 4g; Protein: 11g; Sodium: 136mg

Vegetable Fried Rice

Serves 6 / Prep time: 10 minutes / Cook time: 40 minutes

This dish is equally delicious as a side or main course. You can add edamame or serve it with Tofu Kebabs (page 97) for some extra protein.

2 cups water

1 cup long-grain white rice

Salt and black pepper

1 teaspoon toasted sesame oil

2 large eggs, beaten

1 tablespoon olive oil

1 (1-pound) package frozen mixed vegetables

¼ cup canned unsweetened coconut milk

3 tablespoons soy sauce

1. In a saucepan, bring the water to a boil over medium-high heat. Add the rice, season it with salt and pepper, and bring back to a boil. Lower the heat to low, cover, and cook for 18 minutes. Remove the pan from the heat and let it sit, covered, for 10 minutes.

2. In a large skillet, warm the sesame oil over medium-high heat. Add the eggs and cook until just set, about 3 minutes. Transfer the eggs to a plate and cut them into large pieces.

3. Add the olive oil and mixed vegetables to the skillet. Stir-fry for 4 minutes.

4. Add the rice, coconut milk, soy sauce, and eggs to the skillet and season everything with salt and pepper. Cook, stirring often, until heated through, 5 to 6 minutes.

MAKE AHEAD: Store this fried rice in an airtight container in the refrigerator for up to 4 days.

Per serving: Calories: 237; Total fat: 7g; Carbohydrates: 36g; Fiber: 4g; Protein: 7g; Sodium: 491mg

Egg Flatbreads

Serves 4 / Prep time: 10 minutes / Cook time: 10 minutes

Feel free to play with this one and use whatever veggies or cheese you have on hand. If you'd like to kick up the heat, finish with a drizzle of sriracha.

¼ cup cream cheese, softened

4 naan flatbreads

1½ cups chopped spinach

½ cup seeded and diced tomato

4 slices red onion, centers removed

4 large eggs

¼ teaspoon red pepper flakes

Salt and black pepper

½ cup shredded cheddar cheese

1. Preheat the oven to 425°F.

2. Spread the cream cheese on the flatbreads in a thin layer, leaving a 1-inch border at the edges. Top each flatbread with spinach, tomato, and an onion ring.

3. Crack 1 egg into a small bowl and slide the egg into the center of an onion ring. Repeat with the remaining eggs. Sprinkle the flatbreads with the red pepper flakes and season them with salt and pepper.

4. Sprinkle the flatbreads with the cheddar cheese and bake until the egg whites are set, 10 to 12 minutes.

SUBSTITUTE: Most grocery stores carry naan near the deli depart-ment. If you can't find it, a parbaked pizza crust can be used.

Per serving: Calories: 480; Total fat: 21g; Carbohydrates: 55g; Fiber: 3g; Protein: 19g; Sodium: 1003mg

Veggie Carbonara

Serves 4 / Prep time: 15 minutes / Cook time: 16 minutes

Few foods comfort like a warm bowl of pasta, and this veggie-loaded bowl is my idea of perfection. Add a green salad, and you've got a meal fit for company.

1 pound spaghetti

1 cup frozen baby peas, thawed

1 pound asparagus, trimmed and cut into 1-inch pieces

1 cup halved cherry tomatoes

3 large eggs

½ cup grated vegetarian Parmesan cheese

¼ teaspoon red pepper flakes

Salt and black pepper

¼ cup chopped fresh parsley

1. Bring a large pot of salted water to a boil over high heat. Cook the spaghetti according to the package instructions, adding the peas during the last minute of cooking. Scoop out and reserve ⅓ cup of the cooking water, then drain the pasta. Transfer the pasta and peas to a large bowl and keep them warm.

2. Meanwhile, coat a large skillet with cooking spray and set over medium-high heat. Add the asparagus and sauté for 3 minutes. Add the tomatoes and sauté for 5 minutes longer.

3. In a medium bowl, whisk together the eggs, Parmesan, and red pepper flakes. Season the mixture with salt and pepper. Pour the egg mixture over the pasta and peas, tossing quickly until evenly mixed. Add a little of the reserved pasta water if necessary to thin out the sauce.

4. Add the asparagus and tomatoes to the pasta and toss to combine. Garnish the dish with the parsley.

MAKE AHEAD: Store the carbonara in an airtight container in the refrigerator for up to 2 days. Reheat in a saucepan, adding butter or oil as needed.

Per serving: Calories: 558; Total fat: 8g; Carbohydrates: 99g; Fiber: 8g; Protein: 24g; Sodium: 194mg

Egg Drop Soup

Serves 4 / Prep time: 10 minutes / Cook time: 10 minutes

This simple soup is full of flavor and perfect when you need something to warm you to the bones! Serve it with Vegetable Fried Rice (page 150) for a complete meal.

4 cups vegetable broth

1 garlic clove, minced

1 teaspoon grated fresh ginger

1½ tablespoons soy sauce

1½ tablespoons cornstarch

2 large eggs

1½ teaspoons toasted sesame oil

Salt and black pepper

2 scallions, chopped

1. In a large pot, combine the vegetable broth, garlic, and ginger and bring to a boil over high heat.

2. In a small bowl, whisk together the soy sauce and cornstarch. Add the mixture to the broth and cook for 2 minutes.

3. Lower the heat to medium-low. In a small bowl, whisk together the eggs and sesame oil and slowly pour the egg mixture into the broth, whisking constantly.

4. Season the soup with salt and pepper and garnish it with the scallions.

MAKE AHEAD: You can make this soup through step 2 and store it in an airtight container in the refrigerator for up to 2 days. Add the egg to the simmering broth just before serving.

Per serving: Calories: 80; Total fat: 4g; Carbohydrates: 6g; Fiber: <1g; Protein: 4g; Sodium: 1011mg

Veggie Burgers with Fried Eggs

Serves 4 / Prep time: 20 minutes / Cook time: 15 minutes

The secret to enjoying veggie burgers is to let go of the idea that they are supposed to replicate their meaty counterparts. This one tastes great all on its own.

1 (15-ounce) can chickpeas, drained and rinsed, divided

⅓ cup chopped walnuts

1 onion, finely chopped

1 tablespoon minced garlic

2 tablespoons tomato paste

Salt and black pepper

1 cup bread crumbs

½ cup crumbled goat cheese

6 large eggs, divided

3 tablespoons olive oil, divided

4 brioche buns, toasted

1. Line a plate with parchment paper.

2. In a food processor, process ½ cup chickpeas until smooth. Add the remaining chickpeas and the walnuts and pulse until the chickpeas are mostly mashed but still a little chunky.

3. Coat a large skillet with cooking spray and set it over medium-high heat. Add the onion and sauté for 6 minutes. Add the garlic and sauté for 1 minute. Add the tomato paste, season the mixture with salt and pepper, and stir to combine. Remove the skillet from the heat and stir in the chickpea mixture, bread crumbs, and goat cheese.

4. In a small bowl, whisk 2 eggs. Add them to the chickpea mixture and stir to combine. Form the mixture into 4 patties, place them on the prepared plate, and freeze for 10 minutes.

5. Wipe out the skillet with a paper towel and warm 2 tablespoons olive oil over medium-high heat. Add the patties, cover, and cook until golden, 3 to 6 minutes per side.

6. In another large skillet, warm the remaining 1 tablespoon oil over medium heat. Add the remaining 4 eggs and cook them to your desired doneness, 1 to 3 minutes.

7. Place the patties on the toasted buns and top each with an egg.

MAKE AHEAD: Store the patties in an airtight container in the refrigerator for up to 4 days or in the freezer for up to 3 months, then cook as directed.

Per serving: Calories: 819; Total fat: 41g; Carbohydrates: 85g; Fiber: 10g; Protein: 29g; Sodium: 940mg

Pasta and Pizza

Loaded Mac and Cheese

Serves 10 / Prep time: 20 minutes / Cook time: 35 minutes

In this dish, the rich cheese sauce is balanced with broccoli, carrots, and baby peas. This recipe is highly adaptable, so feel free to use whatever veggies you like.

1 pound elbow macaroni

1 head broccoli, chopped into small florets

1½ cups frozen baby peas, thawed

3 carrots, peeled and grated

2 tablespoons unsalted butter

2 tablespoons all-purpose flour

2 cups milk

2 cups grated cheddar cheese, divided

1 teaspoon ground mustard

¼ teaspoon cayenne pepper

Salt and black pepper

1. Preheat the oven to 350°F. Spray a 9-by-13-inch casserole dish with cooking spray.

2. Bring a large pot of salted water to a boil over high heat. Cook the pasta according to the package directions, adding the broccoli, peas, and carrots in the last 2 minutes. Drain.

3. Meanwhile, in a large saucepan, melt the butter over medium heat. Add the flour and whisk until golden, 2 minutes. Add the milk and cook, stirring often, until the mixture thickens, 8 minutes.

4. Lower the heat to low, add 1½ cups cheese, the mustard, and cayenne, and season the sauce with salt and pepper. Cook, stirring, until the cheese melts.

5. Toss the pasta and vegetables with the cheese sauce and transfer to the prepared casserole dish. Top with the remaining ½ cup cheese.

6. Bake for 25 minutes. Let the mac and cheese sit for 10 minutes before serving.

MAKE AHEAD: Store this dish in an airtight container in the refrigerator for up to 4 days.

Per serving: Calories: 361; Total fat: 13g; Carbohydrates: 47g; Fiber: 5g; Protein: 16g; Sodium: 244mg

Easy Ricotta Pasta

Serves 4 / Prep time: 5 minutes / Cook time: 10 minutes

This dish is shockingly simple to make and loved by kids and adults alike. I often add veggies in the last 2 minutes of the pasta's cooking time—baby peas and spinach are particularly nice here.

8 ounces penne pasta

1 cup ricotta cheese

Juice of 1 lemon

1 teaspoon minced garlic

Salt and black pepper

¼ cup chopped fresh basil

¼ cup toasted pine nuts

1. Bring a large pot of salted water to a boil over high heat. Cook the pasta according to the package directions. Scoop out and reserve ¼ cup of the cooking water, then drain the pasta. Return the pasta to the pot.

2. In a medium bowl, mix together the ricotta, lemon juice, and garlic. Season the cheese mixture with salt and pepper.

3. Add the ricotta mixture and 1 tablespoon of the reserved cooking water to the pasta and stir to combine. Add additional water as needed to achieve the desired consistency.

4. Add the basil, toss, and top the pasta with the pine nuts.

MAKE AHEAD: Store this dish in an airtight container in the refrigerator for up to 3 days. Reheat in a saucepan, adding butter or olive oil as needed.

Per serving: Calories: 361; Total fat: 12g; Carbohydrates: 50g; Fiber: 3g; Protein: 13g; Sodium: 78mg

Roasted Tomato and Ricotta Pasta

Serves 4 / Prep time: 10 minutes / Cook time: 35 minutes

If you are craving something rich and satisfying, this is the dish you should be making. Serve it with fresh lemon wedges for an extra burst of flavor.

1 pint grape tomatoes, halved

2 tablespoons olive oil, divided

8 ounces fettuccini

1 teaspoon minced garlic

5 ounces baby spinach

1 cup half-and-half

Salt and black pepper

1 cup ricotta cheese

¼ cup grated vegetarian Parmesan cheese

⅓ cup chopped fresh basil

1. Preheat the oven to 400°F. Line a rimmed baking sheet with parchment paper.

2. Put the tomatoes on the baking sheet and toss them with 1 tablespoon olive oil. Roast for 20 minutes.

3. Bring a large pot of salted water to a boil over high heat. Cook the pasta according to the package instructions. Scoop out and reserve ½ cup of the cooking water, then drain the pasta.

4. In a large skillet, warm the remaining 1 tablespoon olive oil over medium heat. Add the garlic and spinach and sauté until the spinach is wilted, about 3 minutes. Lower the heat to medium-low, add the half-and-half, and season the mixture with salt and pepper. Cook, stirring, for 5 minutes. Add the ricotta and stir until combined. Add the fettuccine and tomatoes and toss to combine. Add the reserved cooking water, 1 tablespoon at a time, until the desired consistency is reached.

5. Top the pasta with the Parmesan and basil.

MAKE AHEAD: Store this dish in an airtight container in the refrigerator for up to 3 days.

Per serving: Calories: 480; Total fat: 22g; Carbohydrates: 56g; Fiber: 4g; Protein: 16g; Sodium: 210mg

Roasted Red Pepper Penne

Serves 6 / Prep time: 10 minutes / Cook time: 20 minutes

This simple pasta recipe comes together really quickly. Serve it alongside a peppery arugula salad for a complete meal.

1 pound penne pasta

6 roasted red peppers

2 tablespoons olive oil

1 onion, finely chopped

2 teaspoons minced garlic

1 cup vegetable broth

2 teaspoons Italian seasoning

Salt and black pepper

4 ounces fresh mozzarella cheese, diced

⅓ cup grated vegetarian Parmesan cheese

¼ cup chopped fresh basil

1. Bring a large pot of salted water to a boil over high heat. Cook the pasta according to the package instructions. Scoop out and reserve ⅓ cup of the cooking water, then drain the pasta. Return the pasta to the pot.

2. In a food processor, process the red peppers until smooth.

3. In a small saucepan, warm the oil over medium heat. Add the onion and sauté for 5 minutes. Add the garlic and sauté for 1 minute more. Add the red peppers, broth, and Italian seasoning and bring the mixture to a boil. Lower the heat to medium-low and simmer for 4 minutes. Season the sauce with salt and pepper.

4. Add the red pepper sauce to the pasta and toss to combine. Add the reserved cooking water, 1 tablespoon at a time, until the desired consistency is reached.

5. Add the mozzarella and Parmesan to the pasta and stir to combine. Garnish with the basil.

MAKE AHEAD: Store this dish, without the basil, in an airtight container in the refrigerator. Add the basil just before serving.

Per serving: Calories: 423; Total fat: 11g; Carbohydrates: 63g; Fiber: 5g; Protein: 14g; Sodium: 639mg

Mushroom Bolognese

Serves 6 / Prep time: 15 minutes / Cook time: 50 minutes

Mushrooms stand in beautifully for the meat traditionally found in Bolognese sauce and are so satisfying that even meat-eaters will approve.

2 tablespoons olive oil

1 onion, chopped

1½ pounds cremini mushrooms, sliced

1 teaspoon minced garlic

1 (6-ounce) can tomato paste

1 (28-ounce) can crushed tomatoes

½ cup dry red wine

1 teaspoon Italian seasoning

Salt and black pepper

1 pound fettuccine

½ cup half-and-half

½ cup grated vegetarian Parmesan cheese

1. In a large skillet or Dutch oven, warm the olive oil over medium-high heat. Add the onion and mushrooms and sauté until softened, about 15 minutes. Add the garlic and tomato paste and sauté for 1 minute more.

2. Add the crushed tomatoes, red wine, and Italian seasoning. Season the sauce with salt and pepper and bring it to a boil. Lower the heat to low and simmer the sauce until thickened, about 25 minutes.

3. Bring a large pot of salted water to a boil over high heat. Cook the pasta according to the package instructions. Scoop out and reserve ½ cup of the cooking water, then drain the pasta.

4. Add the pasta to the sauce and season it with salt and pepper. Stir in the half-and-half and Parmesan; if necessary, add the reserved cooking water, 1 tablespoon at a time, until you obtain the desired consistency.

MAKE AHEAD: Store the Bolognese in an airtight container in the refrigerator for up to 4 days or in the freezer for up to 3 months.

Per serving: Calories: 487; Total fat: 10g; Carbohydrates: 83g; Fiber: 7g; Protein: 17g; Sodium: 398mg

Garlic Spaghetti

Serves 4 / Prep time: 10 minutes / Cook time: 10 minutes

This pasta delivers an unexpected boldness of flavors. Serve it with Radicchio and Kale Salad (page 41) for a complete meal.

8 ounces spaghetti

¼ cup olive oil

2 tablespoons minced garlic

2 tablespoons freshly squeezed lemon juice

½ teaspoon red pepper flakes

Salt and black pepper

½ cup grated vegetarian Parmesan cheese

¼ cup chopped fresh parsley

¼ cup toasted chopped walnuts

1. Bring a large pot of salted water to a boil over high heat. Cook the pasta according to the package instructions. Scoop out and reserve ¼ cup of the cooking water, then drain the pasta. Return the pasta to the pot.

2. In a large skillet, warm the olive oil over medium-low heat. Add the garlic and sauté for 1 minute. Stir in the lemon juice and red pepper flakes and season the mixture with salt and pepper.

3. Add the pasta and 2 tablespoons of the reserved cooking water to the skillet and toss until all is combined. Add the Parmesan and parsley and stir to combine. Use the remaining reserved cooking water to adjust the consistency if needed.

4. Top the spaghetti with the walnuts.

MAKE AHEAD: Store this garlic spaghetti in an airtight container in the refrigerator for up to 4 days.

Per serving: Calories: 419; Total fat: 21g; Carbohydrates: 49g; Fiber: 3g; Protein: 9g; Sodium: 147mg

Pasta with Pumpkin Alfredo Sauce

Serves 4 / Prep time: 20 minutes / Cook time: 15 minutes

Make this recipe in the fall, when you are craving all things pumpkin. It pairs nicely with a green salad and a loaf of crusty bread in front of a roaring fire.

12 ounces rotini pasta

1 tablespoon unsalted butter

2 shallots, finely chopped

2 teaspoons minced garlic

1 tablespoon all-purpose flour

1½ cups half-and-half

¾ cup canned pumpkin puree

1 cup grated vegetarian Parmesan cheese

Salt and black pepper

1. Bring a large pot of salted water to a boil over high heat. Cook the pasta according to the package instructions. Scoop out and reserve ⅓ cup of the cooking water, then drain the pasta.

2. Meanwhile, in a saucepan, melt the butter over medium heat. Add the shallots and sauté for 5 minutes. Add the garlic and sauté for 1 minute more. Sprinkle the shallots and garlic with the flour and stir.

3. Whisk in the half-and-half and bring the mixture to a simmer, stirring often. Add the pumpkin puree and cook until thickened, about 4 minutes.

4. Lower the heat to low, add the Parmesan, season the sauce with salt and pepper, and cook until the cheese is melted.

5. Toss the pasta with the sauce and add the reserved cooking water, 1 tablespoon at a time, until the desired consistency is reached.

MAKE AHEAD: Store this dish in an airtight container in the refrigerator for up to 4 days.

Per serving: Calories: 583; Total fat: 19g; Carbohydrates: 87g; Fiber: 6g; Protein: 16g; Sodium: 370mg

Spinach Ravioli with Roasted Tomatoes

Serves 4 / Prep time: 15 minutes / Cook time: 30 minutes

Roasting tomatoes brings out their natural sweetness and provides just the right balance for cheesy ravioli.

1 pint grape tomatoes, halved

1 tablespoon olive oil

8 ounces ricotta-spinach ravioli

2 tablespoons unsalted butter

2 shallots, diced

1 teaspoon minced garlic

1 tablespoon all-purpose flour

¾ cup milk

Salt and black pepper

¼ cup grated vegetarian Parmesan cheese

¼ cup chopped fresh basil

1. Preheat the oven to 400°F. Line a rimmed baking sheet with parchment paper.

2. Toss the tomatoes with the olive oil and spread them out in a single layer on the prepared baking sheet. Roast for 20 minutes.

3. Meanwhile, bring a large pot of salted water to a boil over high heat. Cook the ravioli according to the package instructions. Scoop out and reserve ⅓ cup of the cooking water, then drain the pasta.

4. In a large pot, melt the butter over medium-high heat. Add the shallots and sauté for 3 minutes. Add the garlic and sauté for 1 minute more. Sprinkle in the flour, add the milk, season with salt and pepper, and bring to a boil. Lower the heat to medium and simmer, stirring, until thickened, about 3 minutes.

5. Add the ravioli and tomatoes to the shallot-and-garlic mixture and toss to combine. Add the reserved cooking water, 1 tablespoon at a time, until the pasta is the desired consistency.

6. Sprinkle the ravioli with the Parmesan and basil.

MAKE AHEAD: Store this dish in an airtight container in the refrigerator for up to 1 day.

Per serving: Calories: 230; Total fat: 14g; Carbohydrates: 19g; Fiber: 3g; Protein: 6g; Sodium: 268mg

Southwestern Pasta

Serves 4 / Prep time: 10 minutes / Cook time: 15 minutes

This dish packs a punch of flavor. Seeding the jalapeño keeps the heat to a minimum, but you can substitute a poblano pepper to make this more kid-friendly.

8 ounces penne pasta

1 onion, chopped

1 jalapeño, seeded and diced

1 teaspoon minced garlic

1 tablespoon all-purpose flour

1 teaspoon chili powder

1 teaspoon smoked paprika

Salt and black pepper

¾ cup vegetable broth

1 (15-ounce) can black beans, drained and rinsed

2 cups frozen corn, thawed

2 cups quartered cherry tomatoes

1. Bring a large pot of salted water to a boil over high heat. Cook the pasta according to the package instructions. Scoop out and reserve ⅓ cup of the cooking water, then drain the pasta.

2. Meanwhile, coat a large skillet with cooking spray and set it over medium heat. Add the onion and jalapeño and sauté for 7 minutes. Add the garlic and sauté for 1 minute more. Sprinkle in the flour, add the chili powder and smoked paprika, and stir. Season the mixture with salt and pepper.

3. Add the broth, black beans, corn, and cherry tomatoes and bring the mixture to a boil. Lower the heat to medium-low and simmer until thickened, about 3 minutes. Add the pasta and the reserved cooking water, 1 tablespoon at a time, until the pasta is the desired consistency.

MAKE AHEAD: Store this dish in an airtight container in the refrigerator for up to 4 days.

Per serving: Calories: 425; Total fat: 2g; Carbohydrates: 87g; Fiber: 14g; Protein: 17g; Sodium: 152mg

Lasagna for All

Serves 10 / Prep time: 20 minutes / Cook time: 1 hour

Lasagna is my forever favorite when it comes to entertaining family and close friends. This version is always a hit with vegetarians and carnivores alike.

12 ounces lasagna noodles

1 pound zucchini, thinly sliced lengthwise

Salt and black pepper

9 ounces spinach, chopped

3 cups ricotta cheese

½ cup grated vegetarian Parmesan cheese

1 large egg, beaten

2 teaspoons minced garlic

½ cup chopped basil, plus 6 whole leaves

½ teaspoon red pepper flakes

1 (26-ounce) jar marinara sauce

3 cups shredded mozzarella cheese

1. Preheat the oven to 350°F. Coat a 9-by-13-inch baking dish with cooking spray.

2. Bring a large pot of salted water to a boil over high heat. Add the lasagna noodles and cook according to the package instructions. Drain the noodles and place them in a single layer on paper towels.

3. Meanwhile, coat a large skillet with cooking spray and set it over medium heat. Add the zucchini slices to the skillet, season them with salt and pepper, and sauté until tender, 1 to 3 minutes. Transfer the sautéed slices to paper towels to drain.

4. Spray the skillet again, add the spinach, and sauté until it wilts, about 2 minutes. Remove the spinach from the skillet and drain it well, pressing down on it with a paper towel to remove excess moisture.

5. In a medium bowl, mix together the ricotta, spinach, Parmesan, egg, garlic, chopped basil, and red pepper flakes. Season the ricotta mixture with salt and pepper.

continued

6. Spread ¼ cup marinara in the bottom of the prepared baking dish. Create layers with one-third of the noodles, half of the zucchini, half of the ricotta mixture, and half of the mozzarella. Spread one-third of the remaining marinara over the mozzarella. Repeat the layers, then finish with one last layer of noodles and the remaining marinara.

7. Bake for 30 minutes. Let the lasagna cool for 15 minutes, then garnish it with the basil leaves.

MAKE AHEAD: Store this lasagna, tightly covered, in the refrigerator for up to 3 days.

Per serving: Calories: 440; Total fat: 21g; Carbohydrates: 46g; Fiber: 4g; Protein: 22g; Sodium: 772mg

Mediterranean Orzo

Serves 6 / Prep time: 15 minutes / Cook time: 25 minutes

If you love Mediterranean flavors, this dish will have you doing a happy dance. Try serving this with a Greek salad, preferably on a spring evening with a glass of white wine.

½ cup sliced sun-dried tomatoes

1 tablespoon olive oil

1 onion, chopped

1 teaspoon minced garlic

½ teaspoon red pepper flakes

Salt and black pepper

12 ounces orzo

2½ cups vegetable broth

½ cup dry white wine

4 ounces goat cheese, crumbled

1 (14½-ounce) can quartered artichokes, drained and rinsed

⅓ cup diced roasted red peppers

1. Put the sun-dried tomatoes in a small bowl, pour in enough hot water to cover them, and let them sit for 10 minutes. Drain.

2. In a large skillet, warm the olive oil over medium-high heat. Add the onion and sauté for 8 minutes. Add the garlic and red pepper flakes and season with salt and pepper. Add the orzo and sauté for 3 minutes.

3. Add the broth and wine and bring to a boil. Lower the heat to medium-low and simmer until the orzo is al dente, about 12 minutes.

4. Stir in the goat cheese, artichokes, roasted red peppers, and sun-dried tomatoes and cook until heated through, about 3 minutes.

MAKE AHEAD: Store this dish in an airtight container in the refrigerator for up to 3 days.

Per serving: Calories: 363; Total fat: 9g; Carbohydrates: 54g; Fiber: 6g; Protein: 14g; Sodium: 698mg

Mushroom Stroganoff

Serves 4 / Prep time: 10 minutes / Cook time: 15 minutes

Discover the richness of flavors in this incredibly creamy pasta dish. Serve it with a green salad and crusty bread for a complete meal.

8 ounces fettuccine

2 tablespoons olive oil

2 cups sliced button or cremini mushrooms

1 onion, finely chopped

1 tablespoon all-purposed flour

1 teaspoon smoked paprika

¼ teaspoon red pepper flakes

Salt and black pepper

½ cup dry white wine

1 cup sour cream

2 tablespoons chopped fresh parsley

1. Bring a large pot of salted water to a boil over high heat. Add the fettuccine and cook according to the package instructions. Scoop out and reserve ½ cup of the cooking water, then drain the pasta.

2. Meanwhile, in a large skillet, warm the oil over medium heat. Add the mushrooms and onion and sauté until the mushrooms have released most of their liquid, about 8 minutes.

3. Sprinkle in the flour and add the smoked paprika and red pepper flakes. Season the mushroom mixture with salt and pepper and stir to combine.

4. Add the wine and reserved pasta cooking water, bring the sauce to a boil, and cook for 3 minutes. Lower the heat to low, add the sour cream, and cook, stirring, until heated through, about 1 minute longer.

5. Toss the fettuccine with the sauce and top it with the parsley.

MAKE AHEAD: Store this dish in an airtight container in the refrigerator for up to 3 days.

Per serving: Calories: 437; Total fat: 19g; Carbohydrates: 52g; Fiber: 3g; Protein: 11g; Sodium: 27mg

Spinach and Caramelized Onion Bow Tie Pasta

Serves 6 / Prep time: 15 minutes / Cook time: 35 minutes

Sometimes I dream about this dish and the next day I have to make it so I can enjoy its rich flavors. While I love bow tie pasta here, any short pasta shape will do.

2 tablespoons olive oil

3 onions, coarsely chopped

12 ounces bow tie pasta

5 ounces baby spinach

4 tablespoons unsalted butter

⅔ cup crumbled goat cheese

¼ teaspoon red pepper flakes

Salt and black pepper

1. In a large skillet, warm the oil over medium-high heat. Add the onions and sauté for 5 minutes. Lower the heat to medium-low and cook, stirring occasionally, until the onions are soft and caramelized, 20 to 30 minutes.

2. Meanwhile, bring a large pot of salted water to a boil over high heat. Cook the pasta according to the package instructions, adding the spinach during the last minute of cooking. Scoop out and reserve ½ cup of the cooking water, then drain the pasta and spinach.

3. Add the butter to the onions and stir to combine. Add the pasta and spinach, goat cheese, and red pepper flakes to the skillet and season all with salt and pepper. Toss the pasta to coat it evenly with the sauce, then add the reserved cooking water, 1 tablespoon at a time, until it reaches the desired consistency.

MAKE AHEAD: Store this dish in an airtight container in the refrigerator for up to 4 days.

Per serving: Calories: 403; Total fat: 18g; Carbohydrates: 49g; Fiber: 3g; Protein: 12g; Sodium: 149mg

Buddha Bowls

Serves 4 / Prep time: 15 minutes / Cook time: 8 minutes

Looking for something that makes meal prep really easy? These pasta bowls are ideal for packing into individual containers for grab-and-go lunches.

8 ounces soba or black rice noodles

⅓ cup peanut butter

1 tablespoon soy sauce

1 tablespoon freshly squeezed lime juice

2 teaspoons maple syrup

1 cup shelled cooked edamame

1 cup bean sprouts

1 cup shredded purple cabbage

3 carrots, peeled and cut into matchsticks

1 red bell pepper, seeded and chopped

Thinly sliced scallions, for serving

Chopped roasted peanuts, for serving

1. Bring a large pot of salted water to a boil over high heat. Cook the noodles according to the package instructions. Scoop out and reserve ⅓ cup of the cooking water, then drain the pasta. Rinse the pasta under cold running water, then drain it again.

2. In a small bowl, whisk together the reserved cooking water and peanut butter. Add the soy sauce, lime juice, and maple syrup and stir to combine.

3. Divide the noodles among 4 serving bowls. Top each bowl with one-quarter of the edamame, bean sprouts, purple cabbage, carrots, and bell pepper. Drizzle the bowls with the peanut sauce, then sprinkle them with scallions and peanuts.

MAKE AHEAD: Store this dish in an airtight container in the refrigerator for up to 4 days. If you will not be serving them right away, I recommend tossing the noodles with a bit of olive oil to keep them from sticking together.

Per serving: Calories: 420; Total fat: 13g; Carbohydrates: 63g; Fiber: 5g; Protein: 20g; Sodium: 722mg

Spicy Thai-Inspired Bowls

Serves 4 / Prep time: 10 minutes / Cook time: 12 minutes

Loaded with veggies and tossed with a punchy sauce, this is a dish that never gets old. For extra flavor, finish these bowls with chopped fresh cilantro and sesame seeds.

¼ cup peanut butter

¼ cup soy sauce

2 tablespoons freshly squeezed lime juice

2 tablespoons rice vinegar

3 tablespoons toasted sesame oil, divided

1 tablespoon sriracha

2 teaspoons minced garlic

Salt and black pepper

8 ounces pad Thai noodles

2 cups chopped broccoli florets

2 carrots, peeled and shredded

1 red bell pepper, seeded and cut into strips

1. In a blender, combine the peanut butter, soy sauce, lime juice, rice vinegar, 1 tablespoon sesame oil, sriracha, and garlic. Season the mixture with salt and pepper and process until smooth.

2. Bring a large pot of salted water to a boil over high heat. Cook the noodles according to the package instructions. Drain the noodles and transfer them to a large bowl. Add the peanut sauce and toss to combine.

3. In a skillet, warm the remaining 2 tablespoons sesame oil over medium heat. Add the broccoli and stir-fry for 2 minutes. Add the carrots and bell pepper and stir-fry for 2 minutes. Add the vegetables to the pasta and toss to combine.

MAKE AHEAD: Store this dish in an airtight container in the refrigerator for up to 4 days.

Per serving: Calories: 441; Total fat: 19g; Carbohydrates: 59g; Fiber: 5g; Protein: 10g; Sodium: 1032mg

Sun-Dried Tomato and Broccoli Alfredo

Serves 6 / Prep time: 10 minutes / Cook time: 15 minutes

Alfredo pasta is my idea of comfort food. I like to finish it with a squeeze of fresh lemon juice to brighten the dish and highlight the vegetables.

12 ounces fettuccine

2 cups broccoli florets

1 cup chopped sun-dried tomatoes

4 tablespoons unsalted butter

2 shallots, minced

1 teaspoon minced garlic

1 tablespoon all-purpose flour

2 cups milk

3 ounces cream cheese, cubed

Salt and black pepper

¾ cup grated vegetarian Parmesan cheese

1. Bring a large pot of salted water to a boil over high heat. Cook the pasta according to the package instructions, adding the broccoli and sun-dried tomatoes to the pot during the last 3 minutes of cooking. Scoop out and reserve ½ cup of the cooking water, then drain the pasta and vegetables.

2. Meanwhile, in a large saucepan, melt the butter over medium heat. Add the shallots and sauté for 3 minutes. Add the garlic and sauté for 1 minute more. Sprinkle in the flour and stir to combine. Add the milk and cream cheese and cook, whisking, until the cheese is melted. Season the sauce with salt and pepper.

3. Lower the heat to low. Add the Parmesan and stir until it is melted. Add the pasta and vegetables and toss to combine. Add the reserved cooking water, 1 tablespoon at a time, until the pasta is the desired consistency.

MAKE AHEAD: Store this dish in an airtight container in the refrigerator for up to 3 days.

Per serving: Calories: 482; Total fat: 20g; Carbohydrates: 63g; Fiber: 4g; Protein: 13g; Sodium: 426mg

Three-Cheese Pizza

Serves 8 / Prep time: 2 hours / Cook time: 20 minutes

My seven-year-old would happily eat this recipe seven nights a week if I'd let her. This recipe makes 2 pizzas.

For the pizza dough

1 cup warm water (105°F to 110°F)

2½ teaspoons active dry yeast

1 teaspoon sugar

3 cups bread flour, plus more for dusting

1 teaspoon sea salt

3 tablespoons olive oil, plus more for the bowl

For the toppings

½ cup marinara sauce

1 cup shredded mozzarella cheese

1 cup shredded sharp cheddar cheese

½ cup grated vegetarian Parmesan cheese

To make the pizza dough

1. Place a pizza stone on the bottom rack of the oven and preheat the oven and stone to 425°F.

2. In a small bowl, whisk together the warm water, yeast, and sugar and let the yeast mixture sit in a warm place until it is foamy, 5 to 10 minutes.

3. In the bowl of a stand mixer fitted with the dough hook, combine the flour and salt. Turn the mixer to low and add the yeast mixture and oil. Turn the mixer to medium-high and mix for 4 minutes. Transfer the dough to an oiled bowl and coat it with more oil. Cover the dough with a dish towel and set it in a warm place for 1 hour 30 minutes.

4. Punch down the dough and turn it out onto a floured work surface. Divide the dough into 2 balls and press or roll each into a large circle. Crimp the edges of each circle with your fingers and prick the center of each with a fork.

5. Carefully transfer one dough circle to the pizza stone and bake it for 5 minutes. Repeat with the remaining dough circle.

To assemble the toppings

6. Spread half of the marinara on each crust and top each pizza with half of the mozzarella, cheddar, and Parmesan.

7. Bake for 10 to 15 minutes, until the cheeses are melted and the crusts are browned.

MAKE AHEAD: The dough can be stored in a zip-top plastic bag in the refrigerator for up to 5 days or in the freezer for up to 2 months. Store leftovers, tightly wrapped, in the refrigerator for up to 1 week.

Per serving: Calories: 372; Total fat: 16g; Carbohydrates: 43g; Fiber: 2g; Protein: 14g; Sodium: 635mg

Blue Cheese, Spinach, and Sun-Dried Tomato Pizza

Serves 6 / Prep time: 15 minutes / Cook time: 20 minutes

When you are craving something different, it doesn't get any better than this robust pizza. Goat cheese also tastes amazing here.

1 cup chopped sun-dried tomatoes

½ recipe Pizza Dough (page 178), unbaked

5 ounces baby spinach

3 garlic cloves, thinly sliced

½ cup crumbled blue cheese

¼ cup chopped walnuts

¼ cup grated vegetarian Parmesan cheese

2 tablespoons thinly sliced fresh basil

1. Place a pizza stone on the bottom rack of the oven and preheat the oven and stone to 425°F.

2. Put the sun-dried tomatoes in a small bowl, pour in enough hot water to cover them, and let them sit for 10 minutes. Drain.

3. Roll out the dough on a lightly floured sheet of parchment paper. Crimp the edges with your fingers and prick the center several times with a fork. Carefully transfer the dough to the pizza stone and bake for 5 minutes.

4. Meanwhile, coat a skillet with cooking spray and set it over medium heat. Add the spinach and sauté until wilted, 1 to 2 minutes. Remove the spinach from the skillet and drain it, pressing down on it with a paper towel to remove excess moisture.

5. Scatter the spinach, sun-dried tomatoes, garlic, blue cheese, walnuts, and Parmesan over the crust. Carefully transfer the pizza to the pizza stone and bake until the crust is golden, 15 to 20 minutes. Garnish the pizza with the basil.

MAKE AHEAD: Store leftovers, tightly wrapped, in the refrigerator for up to 3 days.

Per serving: Calories: 275; Total fat: 12g; Carbohydrates: 35g; Fiber: 3g; Protein: 10g; Sodium: 403mg

Caprese Pizza

Serves 4 / Prep time: 20 minutes / Cook time: 45 minutes

This is cheese pizza all grown up. I frequently make a Three-Cheese Pizza (page 178) for the kids and this one for the adults.

1 pint cherry tomatoes, halved

3 garlic cloves, sliced

1½ tablespoons olive oil, divided

½ recipe Pizza Dough (page 178), unbaked

4 ounces fresh mozzarella cheese, sliced

½ teaspoon red pepper flakes

2 teaspoons balsamic glaze

¼ cup thinly sliced fresh basil

1. Place a pizza stone on the bottom rack of the oven and preheat the oven and stone to 425°F. Line a rimmed baking sheet with parchment paper.

2. Toss the tomatoes and garlic with 1 tablespoon olive oil and spread them out in a single layer on the prepared baking sheet. Roast for 25 minutes.

3. Meanwhile, roll out the dough on a lightly floured piece of parchment paper. Crimp the edges with your fingers and prick the center several times with a fork. Carefully transfer the dough to the pizza stone and bake it for 5 minutes.

4. Brush the crust with the remaining ½ tablespoon olive oil. Top it with the roasted tomato mixture and sprinkle it with the mozzarella and red pepper flakes.

5. Bake for 15 to 20 minutes, until the cheese melts and the crust is golden brown. Drizzle the pizza with the balsamic glaze and top it with basil.

MAKE AHEAD: Store leftovers, tightly wrapped, in the refrigerator for up to 1 week.

Per serving: Calories: 385; Total fat: 17g; Carbohydrates: 43g; Fiber: 3g; Protein: 13g; Sodium: 385mg

Spinach Stuffed Shells

Serves 4 / Prep time: 20 minutes / Cook time: 40 minutes

When I want serious comfort food and don't want to spend all day in the kitchen, I make these shells.

8 ounces jumbo pasta shells

2 cups ricotta cheese

1 (15-ounce) package frozen chopped spinach, thawed and squeezed dry

½ cup grated vegetarian Parmesan cheese

2 large eggs, beaten

1 teaspoon minced garlic

1 teaspoon Italian seasoning

Salt and black pepper

1½ cups marinara sauce

1 cup shredded mozzarella cheese

1. Preheat the oven to 350°F.

2. Bring a large pot of salted water to a boil over high heat. Cook the pasta shells according to the package instructions. Drain and rinse the shells under cool water.

3. In a medium bowl, mix together the ricotta, spinach, Parmesan, eggs, garlic, and Italian seasoning. Season the mixture with salt and pepper.

4. Spread 1 cup marinara in the bottom of a 9-by-13-inch baking dish. Stuff the pasta shells with the ricotta mixture and arrange them in the baking dish on top of the marinara. Drizzle the shells with the remaining ½ cup marinara and top them with the mozzarella cheese.

5. Bake for 25 to 30 minutes, until the cheese is melted and bubbly. Let the shells cool for 10 minutes before serving.

MAKE AHEAD: This recipe can be assembled without the mozzarella, covered, and stored in the refrigerator for up to 4 days. Add the mozzarella on top just before baking.

Per serving: Calories: 647; Total fat: 28g; Carbohydrates: 71g; Fiber: 7g; Protein: 32g; Sodium: 971mg

Roasted Vegetable Baked Ziti

Serves 6 / Prep time: 20 minutes / Cook time: 50 minutes

Baked ziti is like a hug in a casserole dish, because cheesy goodness just never gets old. Assemble it ahead of time and bake it just before serving for a luscious main course.

2 zucchini, trimmed and cut into 1-inch cubes

1 small eggplant, peeled and cut into 1-inch cubes

1 onion, cut into wedges

1 red bell pepper, seeded and cut into 1-inch pieces

2 tablespoons olive oil

12 ounces ziti

1 cup ricotta cheese

2 cups shredded mozzarella cheese

1 (26-ounce) jar marinara sauce

½ cup grated vegetarian Parmesan cheese

1. Preheat the oven to 400°F. Line a rimmed baking sheet with parchment paper. Coat a 9-by-13-inch baking dish with cooking spray.

2. Arrange the zucchini, eggplant, onion, and bell pepper in a single layer on the prepared baking sheet and drizzle the vegetables with the olive oil. Season with salt and pepper. Roast for 20 to 25 minutes, until lightly charred.

3. Meanwhile, bring a large pot of salted water to a boil over high heat. Cook the pasta according to the package instructions. Drain the pasta and return it to the pot.

4. Add the ricotta and 1 cup mozzarella to the pasta and stir to combine. Transfer the mixture to the prepared baking dish. Top the pasta with the vegetable mixture and the marinara. Sprinkle the Parmesan and the remaining 1 cup mozzarella over the top.

5. Bake for 25 minutes.

MAKE AHEAD: Store this dish in an airtight container in the refrigerator for up to 4 days.

Per serving: Calories: 597; Total fat: 24g; Carbohydrates: 73g; Fiber: 8g; Protein: 25g; Sodium: 925mg

Linguine Primavera

Serves 6 / Prep time: 10 minutes / Cook time: 15 minutes

With a creamy Parmesan sauce and a kick from garlic and red pepper flakes, this little gem fits right in on a lazy Sunday afternoon.

8 ounces linguine

2 tablespoons olive oil

1 red onion, diced

1 teaspoon minced garlic

¼ teaspoon red pepper flakes

1½ cups halved grape tomatoes

2 carrots, peeled and cut into matchsticks

2 cups frozen baby peas, thawed

¼ cup dry white wine

¾ cup half-and-half

⅓ cup grated vegetarian Parmesan cheese

2 tablespoons chopped fresh thyme or 2 teaspoons dried thyme

1. Bring a large pot of salted water to a boil over high heat. Cook the pasta according to the package instructions. Scoop out and reserve ½ cup of the cooking water, then drain the pasta.

2. Meanwhile, in a skillet, warm the olive oil over medium heat. Add the onion and sauté for 5 minutes. Add the garlic and red pepper flakes and sauté for 1 minute more. Add the tomatoes and carrots and sauté for 3 minutes. Add the peas and sauté for another 1 minute. Add the wine and cook, scraping up the brown bits from the bottom of the skillet, until the wine has evaporated.

3. Add the half-and-half and cook for 2 minutes. Lower the heat to low, add the Parmesan, and cook until the Parmesan has melted and the sauce has thickened. Add the pasta and toss to coat it evenly with the sauce. Garnish the pasta with the thyme.

MAKE AHEAD: Store this dish in an airtight container in the refrigerator for up to 3 days.

Per serving: Calories: 300; Total fat: 10g; Carbohydrates: 43g; Fiber: 5g; Protein: 9g; Sodium: 156mg

Fig Focaccia

Serves 8 / Prep time: 1 hour / Cook time: 30 minutes

While it bakes, this focaccia will fill your kitchen with a delicious aroma. If you can't find figs, it's just as good on its own with salt and rosemary.

¾ cup warm water (105°F to 110°F)

1 tablespoon active dry yeast

1 tablespoon sugar

1¾ cups bread flour, plus more for dusting

1 teaspoon sea salt

1 large egg, at room temperature

6 tablespoons olive oil, divided

6 fresh figs, sliced

1 teaspoon fresh rosemary leaves

1. Line a rimmed baking sheet with parchment paper.

2. In a small bowl, whisk together the water, yeast, and sugar and let it sit in a warm place, 5 to 10 minutes.

3. In the bowl of a stand mixer fitted with the dough hook, combine the flour and salt.

4. In a small bowl, beat the egg and add 5 tablespoons olive oil. Add the yeast mixture and mix well. Add to the flour and beat on medium-high for 4 minutes.

5. Transfer the dough to the prepared baking sheet and carefully press the dough down out to the edges, adding flour as needed to keep your hands from sticking.

6. Brush the dough with the remaining 1 tablespoon olive oil. Cover it with a kitchen towel and let it rise in a warm place for 35 minutes. Preheat the oven to 400°F.

7. Arrange the figs over the dough, scatter with fresh rosemary, and bake for 25 to 30 minutes, until golden. Cool on a wire rack.

MAKE AHEAD: Store this focaccia, wrapped in plastic wrap, at room temperature for up to 2 days.

Per serving: Calories: 245; Total fat: 11g; Carbohydrates: 31g; Fiber: 2g; Protein: 5g; Sodium: 301mg

Mediterranean Hummus Pasta

Serves 6 / Prep time: 15 minutes / Cook time: 10 minutes

You will love the flavor payoff in this dish, especially when you realize how easy it is to make. Serve a simple Greek salad on the side and have dinner ready in less than 30 minutes.

1 pound cavatappi or elbow macaroni

½ cup sliced sun-dried tomatoes

1 cup hummus

¼ cup vegetable broth

2 tablespoons red wine vinegar

Salt and black pepper

½ red onion, thinly sliced

½ cup sliced pitted olives

½ cup thinly sliced fresh basil

¼ cup toasted pine nuts

1. Bring a large pot of salted water to a boil over high heat. Cook the pasta according to the package directions. Scoop out and reserve 1 cup of the cooking water, then drain the pasta.

2. Meanwhile, put the sun-dried tomatoes in a small bowl, pour in enough hot water to cover them, and let them sit for 10 minutes. Drain.

3. In a medium bowl, whisk together the hummus, vegetable broth, and red wine vinegar. Season the mixture with salt and pepper.

4. Toss the hummus mixture with the pasta. Add the reserved cooking water, 1 tablespoon at a time, until the pasta is the desired consistency. Add the onion, olives, and sun-dried tomatoes and toss to combine. Top with the basil and pine nuts.

MAKE AHEAD: Store this dish in an airtight container in the refrigerator for up to 4 days.

Per serving: Calories: 441; Total fat: 11g; Carbohydrates: 69g; Fiber: 7g; Protein: 14g; Sodium: 271mg

Pecan Pesto Pasta

Serves 6 / Prep time: 10 minutes / Cook time: 10 minutes

Make this scrumptious dish when basil is at the height of its season. Pecans may not be the first nut you think of when it comes to pesto, but their rich, buttery flavor will win you over.

1 pound penne pasta

2 cups chopped fresh basil

½ cup grated vegetarian Parmesan cheese

⅓ cup toasted pecans

1 teaspoon minced garlic

½ cup extra-virgin olive oil

2 tablespoons freshly squeezed lemon juice

Salt and black pepper

1. Bring a large pot of salted water to a boil over high heat. Cook the pasta according to the package instructions. Scoop out and reserve ⅓ cup of the cooking water, then drain the pasta.

2. In a food processor, combine the basil, Parmesan, pecans, and garlic and pulse to combine. Add the olive oil and lemon juice, season the pesto with salt and pepper, and process until smooth. Toss the warm pasta with the pesto.

MAKE AHEAD: Store the pesto in an airtight container in the refrigerator for up to 4 days. Store the pasta and pesto combined in an airtight container in the refrigerator for up to 2 days.

Per serving: Calories: 508; Total fat: 25g; Carbohydrates: 61g; Fiber: 3g; Protein: 11g; Sodium: 99mg

Artichoke "Crab" Cakes

Serves 4 / Prep time: 20 minutes / Cook time: 10 minutes

These delicious little patties are flavor-packed and really scratch any itch you might have for crab cakes. Serve with tartar sauce or cocktail sauce and lemon wedges.

1 cup oyster crackers

1 (28-ounce) can artichoke hearts, drained

1 celery stalk, finely chopped

2 tablespoons chopped fresh parsley

Salt and black pepper

2 large eggs, beaten

2½ tablespoons mayonnaise

2 teaspoons Dijon mustard

2 teaspoons Old Bay seasoning

3 tablespoons olive oil

1. In a food processor, pulse the crackers until they resemble coarse flour.

2. Add the artichoke hearts to the food processor and pulse until they are well chopped but still a little chunky. Transfer the mixture to a large bowl. Add the celery and parsley to the artichoke mixture, season it with salt and pepper, and stir to combine.

3. Add the eggs, mayonnaise, mustard, and Old Bay seasoning and stir to combine. Form the mixture into 4 patties.

4. In a large skillet, warm the olive oil over medium heat. Put the patties in the skillet and cook until crispy and browned, about 4 minutes per side.

MAKE AHEAD: Store these patties in an airtight container in the refrigerator for up to 2 days, then brown them in a skillet when ready to serve.

Per serving: Calories: 315; Total fat: 20g; Carbohydrates: 28g; Fiber: 16g; Protein: 11g; Sodium: 1924mg

Sweet Potato and Quinoa Casserole

Serves 6 / Prep time: 15 minutes / Cook time: 1 hour 10 minutes

This is the perfect one-dish meal. It works equally well for an easy weeknight dinner as it does for entertaining. Just don't expect leftovers.

5 cups diced peeled sweet potatoes

1 tablespoon olive oil, divided

Salt and black pepper

1 onion, diced

1 red bell pepper, seeded and diced

1 teaspoon dried thyme

1 tablespoon minced garlic

1 cup quinoa, rinsed

1¾ cups vegetable broth

2 large eggs

½ cup milk

1 cup grated Gruyère cheese

1. Preheat the oven to 400°F. Coat an 8-inch square baking dish with cooking spray.

2. In a medium bowl, toss the sweet potatoes with ½ tablespoon olive oil. Season with salt and pepper. Spread in a single layer on a parchment-lined baking sheet. Bake for 12 minutes. Lower the oven temperature to 350°F.

3. In a large skillet heat the remaining ½ tablespoon olive oil over medium-high, add the onion, bell pepper, and thyme and sauté for 6 minutes.

4. Add the garlic and quinoa and cook for 1 minute. Add the broth, season with salt and pepper, and bring to a boil. Cover and cook over low heat, 20 to 25 minutes. Stir and remove from the heat. Let sit, covered, for 5 minutes.

5. Transfer the quinoa and sweet potatoes to the baking dish. In a small bowl, whisk together the eggs and milk and pour it over the quinoa. Top with cheese.

6. Bake for 30 minutes. Turn on the broiler and broil for 2 minutes, until browned.

MAKE AHEAD: Store this dish, covered, in the refrigerator for up to 4 days or in the freezer for up to 2 months.

Per serving: Calories: 444; Total fat: 12g; Carbohydrates: 68g; Fiber: 9g; Protein: 16g; Sodium: 472mg

Peanut Tofu Stir-Fry

Serves 4 / Prep time: 30 minutes / Cook time: 30 minutes

Filled with protein-packed tofu, this meal never fails to satisfy. Feel free to vary the vegetables—green beans, snow peas, and mushrooms all work nicely here.

1 cup quinoa, rinsed

1¾ cups water

1 (14-ounce) package extra-firm tofu

3 tablespoons soy sauce, divided

1 tablespoon unseasoned rice vinegar

2 tablespoons dry sherry

2 teaspoons cornstarch

1 teaspoon light brown sugar

2 tablespoons peanut oil

1 bunch scallions, whites roughly chopped and greens thinly sliced

1 (1-inch) piece ginger, peeled and thinly sliced

1 small head napa cabbage, thinly sliced

2 tablespoons chopped peanuts

1. In a saucepan, toast the quinoa over medium heat for 4 minutes. Add the water, cover, and cook over low heat, about 25 minutes. Remove from the heat and let it sit, covered, for 5 minutes.

2. Meanwhile, place the tofu between two layers of paper towels on a plate. Top with another plate and a heavy book. Let drain for 10 minutes.

3. In a shallow bowl, mix 1 tablespoon soy sauce and rice vinegar. Cut the tofu into 1-inch cubes, add to the bowl and let sit for 15 minutes.

4. In a small bowl, mix together the sherry, 2 tablespoons soy sauce, cornstarch, and brown sugar. Set the sauce aside.

5. In a large nonstick skillet, warm the peanut oil over medium heat. Add the tofu and stir-fry until browned, 8 minutes. Add the scallion whites, ginger, and cabbage and stir-fry for 3 to 5 minutes. Add the sauce and cook to thicken, about 1 minute.

6. Divide the quinoa among 4 serving bowls. Top with the tofu, scallion greens, and chopped peanuts.

MAKE AHEAD: Store the quinoa in an airtight container in the refrigerator for up to 6 days.

Per serving: Calories: 404; Total fat: 17g; Carbohydrates: 44g; Fiber: 8g; Protein: 22g; Sodium: 712mg

Teriyaki Tofu

Serves 4 / Prep time: 45 minutes / Cook time: 1 hour 15 minutes

A combination of sweet and savory flavors gives this tofu tons of pizzazz. Make it a meal with a side of rice and roasted green beans.

¼ cup packed light brown sugar

¼ cup mirin

¼ cup soy sauce

Salt and black pepper

1 (14-ounce) package extra-firm tofu

¼ cup chopped fresh cilantro

1. In a saucepan, combine the brown sugar, mirin, and soy sauce and bring the mixture to a boil over medium heat. Lower the heat to medium-low and simmer for 45 minutes. Season the sauce with salt and pepper.

2. Line a plate with a double layer of paper towels. Place the tofu on the plate. Top with another double layer of paper towels and another plate. Place something heavy (such as a few cans of tomatoes) on the top plate and let the tofu drain for 10 minutes.

3. Cut the tofu into 1-inch cubes and put them in a shallow dish. Pour half of the sauce over the tofu and let it sit at room temperature for at least 30 minutes. Drain.

4. Preheat the oven to 400°F. Line a rimmed baking sheet with parchment paper.

5. Spread out the tofu cubes on the prepared baking sheet and bake them for 15 minutes. Turn the tofu cubes over and bake them for another 15 minutes.

6. Serve the tofu with the remaining sauce and topped with the cilantro.

MAKE AHEAD: Marinate the tofu in an airtight container in the refrigerator up to 1 day head.

Per serving: Calories: 179; Total fat: 5g; Carbohydrates: 25g; Fiber: 1g; Protein: 12g; Sodium: 1039mg

Turmeric Tempeh and Quinoa

Serves 4 / Prep time: 15 minutes / Cook time: 1 hour

You will love this amazingly aromatic dish, which is bursting with flavor. Turmeric gives the tempeh its deep color. Feel free to add sautéed spinach or broccoli to the mix.

1 (1-pound) package tempeh

2 tablespoons olive oil, divided

1 teaspoon ground turmeric

Salt and black pepper

1 onion, chopped

1½ teaspoons grated fresh ginger

1 teaspoon minced garlic

2 tomatoes, chopped

¾ teaspoon curry powder

1 cup quinoa, rinsed

1¾ cups vegetable broth

1. Place a steamer basket in a large pot, pour in 2 inches of water, and bring it to a boil over high heat. Lower the heat to medium, add the tempeh, cover, and steam for 10 minutes.

2. In a Dutch oven, warm 1 tablespoon olive oil over medium heat. Add the tempeh, sprinkle it with the turmeric, and season it with salt and pepper. Cook until golden, about 4 minutes per side. Transfer the tempeh to a cutting board and cut it into cubes.

3. Warm the remaining 1 tablespoon olive oil in the Dutch oven. Add the onion and ginger and sauté for 8 minutes. Add the garlic, tomatoes, curry powder, and quinoa, season the mixture with salt and pepper, and sauté for 3 minutes.

4. Add the tempeh cubes and vegetable broth and bring the mixture to a boil. Reduce the heat to low, cover, and cook for 25 minutes. Remove the dish from the heat and let it sit, covered, for 5 minutes before serving.

MAKE AHEAD: Store this dish in an airtight container in the refrigerator for up to 3 days.

Per serving: Calories: 505; Total fat: 20g; Carbohydrates: 49g; Fiber: 18g; Protein: 33g; Sodium: 293mg

Southwest-Style Fajitas

Serves 4 / Prep time: 45 minutes / Cook time: 20 minutes

Deliciously seasoned vegetables are perfectly cooked and then wrapped in warm tortillas and topped off with your favorite fixings. I like to serve these with salsa, sliced avocado, sour cream, and shredded cheese.

¼ cup plus 1 tablespoon olive oil

Juice of 1 lime

1 tablespoon taco seasoning or Southwestern seasoning

Salt and black pepper

1 large red onion, thinly sliced

3 bell peppers, any color, seeded and cut into strips

8 ounces button or cremini mushrooms, sliced

1 zucchini, trimmed and cut into matchsticks

2 garlic cloves, minced

8 corn tortillas

1. In a shallow bowl, whisk together ¼ cup olive oil, the lime juice, and taco seasoning. Season the marinade with salt and pepper. Transfer half of the marinade to another shallow bowl.

2. Put the onion and bell peppers in one bowl and the mushrooms and zucchini in the other bowl; toss the veggies in each bowl to coat them evenly with the marinade. Let the vegetables marinate at room temperature for 30 minutes, then drain them.

3. In a large skillet, warm the remaining 1 tablespoon olive oil over medium-high heat. Add the onion and bell peppers and stir-fry for 6 minutes. Add the mushrooms, zucchini, and garlic and stir-fry for 5 more minutes.

4. In another skillet, cook the tortillas over medium-high heat, a few at a time, until warmed through, about 2 minutes per side. Place 2 tortillas on each plate and top with the vegetables.

MAKE AHEAD: You can marinate the vegetables, covered, in the refrigerator for up to 1 day.

Per serving: Calories: 324; Total fat: 19g; Carbohydrates: 37g; Fiber: 7g; Protein: 7g; Sodium: 192mg

Eggplant Moussaka

Serves 6 / Prep time: 45 minutes / Cook time: 1 hour 30 minutes

If you have never had moussaka, you are in for a treat. With two sauces, this recipe is a bit more work than most, but I promise you will be richly rewarded for your efforts.

2 medium eggplants, peeled and sliced lengthwise into ¼-inch-thick slices

Salt and black pepper

4 tablespoons unsalted butter, divided

1 onion, diced

1 teaspoon minced garlic

1 (28-ounce) can crushed tomatoes

½ teaspoon ground cinnamon

2 tablespoons all-purpose flour

1½ cups milk, at room temperature

⅓ cup grated vegetarian Parmesan cheese

1. Preheat the oven to 400°F. Coat a 9-inch square baking dish with cooking spray.

2. Spread the eggplant on dish towels, sprinkle with salt, and let sit for 30 minutes. Blot dry and place in a single layer on 2 parchment-lined baking sheets. Coat with cooking spray and bake for 25 minutes.

3. In a saucepan, melt 2 tablespoons butter over medium heat. Add the onion and garlic and sauté for 4 minutes. Add the tomatoes and cinnamon, season with salt and pepper, and bring to a boil. Cover and cook over low heat for 30 minutes.

4. In another saucepan, melt the remaining 2 tablespoons butter over medium heat. Add the flour and cook, stirring, for 3 minutes. Whisk in the milk to simmer for 2 minutes. Season with salt and pepper.

5. Arrange half of the eggplant in the baking dish. Layer with tomato sauce, remaining eggplant, cream sauce, and cheese. Bake for 20 to 25 minutes, until bubbling. Let stand for 10 minutes before serving.

MAKE AHEAD: Store this moussaka, covered, in the refrigerator for up to 1 day, then bake as directed.

Per serving: Calories: 231; Total fat: 11g; Carbohydrates: 30g; Fiber: 9g; Protein: 7g; Sodium: 365mg

Sheet Pan Eggplant Stacks

Serves 6 / Prep time: 30 minutes / Cook time: 25 minutes

I've always loved eggplant Parmesan, and this recipe is a fun way to enjoy all of the flavors with a bit less fuss.

⅔ cup all-purpose flour

2 large eggs, beaten

2½ cups Italian
bread crumbs

Salt and black pepper

2 medium eggplants, cut
crosswise into
¼-inch-thick slices

2 large tomatoes, cut into
¼-inch-thick slices

1 cup marinara sauce

8 ounces fresh
mozzarella cheese, sliced

½ cup chopped
fresh basil

1. Preheat the oven to 425°F. Line 2 baking sheets with parchment and coat with cooking spray.

2. Put the flour in a shallow bowl. Beat the eggs in a second shallow bowl. Put the bread crumbs in a third shallow bowl and season with salt and pepper. Dredge the eggplant in the flour, dip into the beaten eggs, and coat in the bread crumbs.

3. Arrange the eggplant in a single layer on one baking sheet and the tomato on the other. Coat with cooking spray and roast for 10 minutes. Flip the eggplant and tomato and continue roasting until the eggplant is browned and the tomatoes are softened, 10 to 15 minutes.

4. When the vegetables are nearly done, warm the marinara sauce in a small saucepan over medium-low heat.

5. On each serving plate, arrange some eggplant slices and top them with tomato slices. Top the tomatoes with the fresh mozzarella and basil. Serve with the warm marinara sauce for dipping.

MAKE AHEAD: Store the breaded eggplant slices, covered, in the refrigerator for up to 1 day, then bake as directed.

Per serving: Calories: 467; Total fat: 14g; Carbohydrates: 64g; Fiber: 11g; Protein: 20g; Sodium: 839mg

Pot Pie

Serves 6 / Prep time: 15 minutes / Cook time: 50 minutes

Creamy and filled with savory goodness, pot pie is always a great choice. Serve a salad on the side to make this a nicely balanced meal.

⅓ cup unsalted butter

1 onion, chopped

8 ounces button or cremini mushrooms, sliced

1 pound russet potatoes, peeled and diced

Salt and black pepper

⅓ cup all-purpose flour

1¾ cups vegetable broth

⅔ cup milk

1 (16-ounce) package frozen peas and carrots, thawed

2 (9-inch) frozen piecrusts, thawed

1. Preheat the oven to 350°F. Coat an 8-inch square baking dish with cooking spray.

2. In a medium saucepan, melt the butter over medium heat. Add the onion and sauté for 5 minutes. Add the mushrooms and potatoes, season them with salt and pepper, and sauté for 6 minutes.

3. Sprinkle in the flour, add the broth and milk, and bring to a boil, stirring constantly. Add the peas and carrots and cook for 2 minutes. Remove the pan from the heat.

4. Roll out one of the piecrusts large enough to cover the bottom and sides of the baking dish, and place it in the dish. Pour the filling over the crust. Roll out the other piecrust into a 9-inch square and place it over the vegetable mixture. Crimp the dough to seal the edges. Cut a slit in the center to vent.

5. Bake for 35 minutes, until golden.

MAKE AHEAD: Store this pot pie, covered, in the refrigerator for up to 2 days.

Per serving: Calories: 504; Total fat: 26g; Carbohydrates: 60g; Fiber: 6g; Protein: 11g; Sodium: 596mg

Cauliflower Tacos

Serves 4 / Prep time: 15 minutes / Cook time: 30 minutes

Taco Tuesday just got veg-friendly, and I think you are going to like it. Experiment with the toppings—sliced avocado or guacamole, diced tomatoes, and sliced red onion are all great options.

1 head cauliflower, cut into florets

2 tablespoons olive oil

3 tablespoons taco seasoning

½ cup sour cream

Grated zest and juice of 1 lime

¼ teaspoon cayenne pepper

Salt and black pepper

8 corn tortillas

½ cup shredded cabbage

½ cup shredded cheddar cheese

½ cup pico de gallo

1. Preheat the oven to 375°F. Line a rimmed baking sheet with parchment paper.

2. Toss the cauliflower with the olive oil and taco seasoning and spread it out in a single layer on the prepared baking sheet. Bake for 25 to 30 minutes, until tender and golden.

3. In a small bowl, mix together the sour cream, lime zest and juice, and cayenne pepper. Season the mixture with salt and pepper.

4. In a skillet, cook the tortillas over medium-high heat, a few at a time, until they are warmed through, about 2 minutes per side.

5. Place 2 tortillas on each plate. Top each with the cauliflower and then the shredded cabbage, cheddar cheese, and pico de gallo. Drizzle the tacos with the sour cream sauce and serve.

MAKE AHEAD: Store the sour cream sauce in an airtight container in the refrigerator for up to 4 days.

Per serving: Calories: 343; Total fat: 19g; Carbohydrates: 38g; Fiber: 7g; Protein: 11g; Sodium: 715mg

Roasted Cauliflower Steaks with Pesto

Serves 4 / Prep time: 10 minutes / Cook time: 40 minutes

Cauliflower is a meaty vegetable that is surprisingly satisfying, particularly when roasted. Serve this with Couscous-Stuffed Tomatoes (page 125) and a green salad for a complete meal.

1 large head cauliflower

½ cup plus 2 tablespoons olive oil, divided

2 cups chopped fresh basil

½ cup grated vegetarian Parmesan cheese

⅓ cup toasted pine nuts

2 tablespoons freshly squeezed lemon juice

1 teaspoon minced garlic

Salt and black pepper

1. Preheat the oven to 400°F. Line a rimmed baking sheet with parchment paper.

2. Trim the bottom of the cauliflower, leaving the stem intact. Cut the cauliflower lengthwise into ¾-inch-thick slices. Brush the slices with 2 tablespoons olive oil and place them in a single layer on the prepared baking sheet.

3. Roast for 30 to 40 minutes, until the steaks are tender and golden brown.

4. In a blender, combine the remaining ½ cup olive oil, basil, Parmesan, pine nuts, lemon juice, and garlic and puree until smooth. Season the pesto with salt and pepper.

5. Place the cauliflower steaks on serving plates and drizzle them with the pesto.

MAKE AHEAD: For extra flavor, you can toss the cauliflower steaks in all but 2 tablespoons of the pesto and marinate them in the refrigerator for up to 2 days before roasting. Use the reserved pesto for drizzling.

Per serving: Calories: 460; Total fat: 43g; Carbohydrates: 17g; Fiber: 6g; Protein: 6g; Sodium: 213mg

Black Bean and Cheese Taquitos

Serves 6 / Prep time: 20 minutes / Cook time: 30 minutes

Get all of the yum and none of the guilt with these baked taquitos. Serve them over crisp romaine lettuce with a dollop of sour cream.

1 zucchini, trimmed and grated

Salt and black pepper

1 (15-ounce) can black beans, drained and rinsed

1 cup frozen corn, thawed

½ cup vegetable broth

3 tablespoons taco seasoning

18 corn tortillas

1 cup shredded cheddar cheese

1. Preheat the oven to 425°F. Line a rimmed baking sheet with parchment paper and coat it with cooking spray.

2. Put the zucchini in a colander and set it over a bowl. Sprinkle it well with salt and let it drain for 10 minutes. Pat the zucchini dry with paper towels.

3. Coat a large skillet with cooking spray and warm it over medium heat. Put the zucchini, black beans, corn, vegetable broth, and taco seasoning in the skillet and season them with salt and pepper. Cook, stirring, for 5 minutes.

4. In another skillet, heat the tortillas, a few at a time, over medium heat for 30 seconds per side. Divide the bean mixture among the tortillas, top it with the cheese, and roll each tortilla tightly into a cigar shape. Place the taquitos, seam-sides down, on the prepared baking sheet. Coat the taquitos with cooking spray.

5. Bake the taquitos for 15 to 18 minutes, until crispy.

MAKE AHEAD: Store the filling in an airtight container in the refrigerator for up to 4 days.

Per serving: Calories: 343; Total fat: 9g; Carbohydrates: 55g; Fiber: 11g; Protein: 14g; Sodium: 525mg

Spanish Rice–Stuffed Peppers

Serves 6 / Prep time: 15 minutes / Cook time: 46 minutes

Depending on the size of the peppers and how tender you prefer them, this family favorite can come together in about 45 minutes. And no need to cover the baking dish when they go in the oven—uncovered, they'll blister up better (as opposed to steaming).

1 tablespoon olive oil

1 onion, diced

2 red bell peppers, seeded and diced

1 teaspoon minced garlic

1½ teaspoons smoked paprika

Salt and black pepper

2¼ cups vegetable broth

1 (8-ounce) package yellow rice

1½ cups frozen baby peas, thawed

1 (14-ounce) can chopped artichoke hearts, drained

⅓ cup chopped pitted green olives

2 tablespoons lemon juice

6 green bell peppers, cored

1. Preheat the oven to 425°F. Coat a 9-by-13-inch baking dish with cooking spray.

2. In a large skillet, warm the olive oil over medium-high heat. Add the onion, red bell peppers, garlic, and smoked paprika, season the veggies with salt and pepper, and sauté for 8 minutes.

3. Add the broth and yellow rice, stir, and bring to a boil. Lower the heat to medium-low, cover, and cook for 18 minutes.

4. Add the peas, artichoke hearts, and green olives and stir to combine. Stir in the lemon juice.

5. Fill the green bell peppers with the rice mixture and place them in the prepared baking dish. Bake for 20 to 30 minutes, until the peppers start to blister.

MAKE AHEAD: Store the rice mixture in an airtight container in the refrigerator for up to 4 days.

Per serving: Calories: 273; Total fat: 4g; Carbohydrates: 53g; Fiber: 11g; Protein: 9g; Sodium: 1263mg

Festive Stuffed Squash

Serves 4 / Prep time: 10 minutes / Cook time: 1 hour 15 minutes

This recipe is short on ingredients and long on flavor. With warm apples and cinnamon-spice flavor, this one will become a go-to for those chilly fall days.

2 large acorn squash, halved and seeded

4 apples, cored, peeled, and chopped

¾ cup dried cranberries

3 tablespoons unsalted butter, melted

3 tablespoons brown sugar

1 teaspoon ground cinnamon

Salt and black pepper

1 tablespoon chopped fresh parsley

1. Preheat the oven to 350°F.

2. Place the squash, cut-sides down, in a large baking dish and roast it for 35 to 45 minutes. Turn the squash halves over and let them sit in the baking dish.

3. In a large bowl, toss together the apples and cranberries. Drizzle the fruit with the melted butter and sprinkle it with the brown sugar and cinnamon. Season the mixture with salt and pepper.

4. Spoon the mixture equally into the squash halves and bake them for 30 to 35 more minutes, until the squash is tender. Top the stuffed squash with the parsley.

MAKE AHEAD: Store the squash, tightly covered, in the refrigerator for up to 2 days.

Per serving: Calories: 377; Total fat: 10g; Carbohydrates: 80g; Fiber: 10g; Protein: 2g; Sodium: 81mg

Buffalo Tofu

Serves 4 / Prep time: 20 minutes / Cook time: 30 minutes

Enjoy all the crispy perfection and flavor of chicken wings with this veg-friendly version made with extra-firm tofu. Serve with ranch or blue cheese dressing for dipping.

1 (14-ounce) package
extra-firm tofu

1 tablespoon olive oil

2 tablespoons cornstarch

1 tablespoon
smoked paprika

Salt and black pepper

½ cup hot sauce

3 tablespoons
unsalted butter

2 tablespoons apple
cider vinegar

1 teaspoon minced garlic

1. Preheat the oven to 400°F. Line a rimmed baking sheet with parchment paper.

2. Line a plate with paper towels. Place the tofu on top, followed by more paper towels, another plate, and a heavy book. Let sit for 10 minutes.

3. Cut the tofu into 1-inch cubes and place in a bowl. Drizzle with olive oil.

4. In a small bowl, mix the cornstarch and paprika and season with salt and pepper. Dust over the tofu cubes until they're coated.

5. Spread the tofu in a single layer on the baking sheet and bake for 15 minutes. Turn the tofu over and bake for another 15 minutes.

6. Meanwhile, in a small saucepan, mix the hot sauce, butter, apple cider vinegar, and garlic and cook over medium heat for 5 minutes.

7. Add the tofu to the sauce and toss well.

MAKE AHEAD: Store the sauce in an airtight container in the refrigerator for up to 4 days.

Per serving: Calories: 225; Total fat: 17g; Carbohydrates: 9g; Fiber: 2g; Protein: 11g; Sodium: 777mg

Southwestern Hash Brown Casserole

Serves 8 / Prep time: 15 minutes / Cook time: 50 minutes

Love fast and easy meals? You'll need just 15 minutes of hands-on time to prepare this classic, comforting casserole.

1 (1-pound) package tempeh

4 tablespoons taco seasoning, divided

1 onion, chopped

1 red bell pepper, seeded and chopped

1 jalapeño, seeded and chopped

1 teaspoon minced garlic

1 (30-ounce) package shredded hash browns

3 cups shredded sharp cheddar cheese, divided

2 (10.5-ounce) cans condensed cream of celery soup

1 cup sour cream

Salt and black pepper

1. Preheat the oven to 350°F. Coat a 9-by-13-inch baking dish with cooking spray.

2. Place a steamer basket in a large pot, pour in 2 inches water, and bring it to a boil. Add the tempeh, cover, and steam for 10 minutes over medium heat. Let cool, then crumble it into pieces.

3. Coat a large skillet with cooking spray. Add the tempeh, 2 tablespoons taco seasoning, onion, bell pepper, and jalapeno and sauté for 8 minutes. Add garlic and cook for 1 minute.

4. In a large bowl, mix together the hash browns, 1 cup cheddar cheese, cream of celery soup, sour cream, and remaining 2 tablespoons taco seasoning. Season the mixture with salt and pepper. Add half to the baking dish.

5. Top hash brown with half of the tempeh and 1 cup cheddar cheese. Layer on the remaining hash browns, tempeh, and remaining 1 cup cheddar cheese.

6. Bake for 30 minutes. Let cool for 10 minutes.

MAKE AHEAD: Store this baked casserole, covered, in the refrigerator for up to 2 days.

Per serving: Calories: 484; Total fat: 26g; Carbohydrates: 38g; Fiber: 12g; Protein: 26g; Sodium: 778mg

Cheese and Black Bean Enchiladas

Serves 6 / Prep time: 15 minutes / Cook time: 35 minutes

To say that I love Mexican food would be an understatement! When I serve this with sour cream, lime wedges, and fresh cilantro, I always do a happy dance.

1 large onion, chopped

1 teaspoon ground cumin

1 teaspoon smoked paprika

Salt and black pepper

1 teaspoon minced garlic

1 (15-ounce) can black beans, drained and rinsed

1 (8-ounce) can diced green chiles, drained

12 corn tortillas

2 cups shredded cheddar cheese, divided

2 cups enchilada sauce

1. Preheat the oven to 350°F. Coat a 9-by-13-inch baking dish with cooking spray.

2. Coat a large skillet with cooking spray and set it over medium heat. Add the onion, cumin, and smoked paprika, season with salt and pepper, and sauté for 6 minutes. Add the garlic and sauté for 1 more minute. Add the black beans and green chiles and stir to combine. Remove the mixture from the heat and stir in 1 cup cheddar cheese.

3. In another skillet, warm the tortillas over medium heat for 30 seconds each. Spoon the black bean and cheese mixture onto the tortillas, roll them up, and arrange them, seam-sides down, in the baking dish. Pour the enchilada sauce over the enchiladas and top them with the remaining 1 cup cheddar cheese.

4. Bake the enchiladas for 25 minutes. Let them cool for 10 minutes.

MAKE AHEAD: Store these baked enchiladas, covered, in the refrigerator for up to 1 day.

Per serving: Calories: 367; Total fat: 15g; Carbohydrates: 44g; Fiber: 9g; Protein: 19g; Sodium: 825mg

Greek Stuffed Peppers

Serves 6 / Prep time: 15 minutes / Cook time: 45 minutes

If you prepare the rice for this dish during your weekly meal prep, you'll be able to make a weeknight dinner in just two easy steps. These stuffed peppers are a big favorite in our house.

1 red onion, chopped

1 teaspoon minced garlic

1 (15-ounce) can diced tomatoes, drained

3 cups cooked brown rice

½ cup chopped pitted olives

½ cup chopped canned artichoke hearts

1 teaspoon dried oregano

Salt and black pepper

6 bell peppers (any color), halved and seeded

½ cup crumbled feta cheese

1. Preheat the oven to 375°F. Line a rimmed baking sheet with parchment paper.

2. Coat a skillet with cooking spray and warm it over medium-high heat. Add the onion and sauté for 6 minutes. Add the garlic and sauté for 1 minute longer. Add the tomatoes, brown rice, olives, artichokes, and oregano, season the mixture with salt and pepper, and stir to combine.

3. Spoon the rice mixture into the bell pepper halves. Place the filled peppers on the prepared baking sheet, stuffing-side up. Top the peppers with the feta.

4. Bake for 35 to 40 minutes, until the peppers are tender.

MAKE AHEAD: Store the filling in an airtight container in the refrigerator for up to 3 days. Store the stuffed peppers, covered, in the refrigerator for up to 1 day, then bake as directed.

Per serving: Calories: 236; Total fat: 6g; Carbohydrates: 40g; Fiber: 7g; Protein: 7g; Sodium: 501mg

Mushroom Wellington

Serves 6 / Prep time: 30 minutes / Cook time: 1 hour 30 minutes

When you serve this impressive main dish, your guests will be thrilled by how great it looks and tastes. I like to use portobello mushrooms for their flavor and texture, but any brown mushrooms will do.

3 tablespoons olive oil, divided

2 onions, chopped

Salt and black pepper

4 cups chopped portobello or cremini mushrooms

10 cups baby spinach

1 teaspoon minced garlic

1 sheet puff pastry, thawed if frozen

1 tablespoon chopped fresh thyme

1 large egg, beaten

1. Preheat the oven to 375°F. Line a rimmed baking sheet with parchment paper.

2. In a large skillet, warm 1 tablespoon olive oil over medium-high heat. Add the onions, season them with salt and pepper, and sauté for 8 minutes. Lower the heat to medium-low and cook, stirring occasionally, for 25 to 30 minutes. Remove the skillet from the heat.

3. Add 1 tablespoon oil to the same skillet and warm it over medium-high heat. Add the mushrooms and sauté for 10 minutes.

4. Add the remaining 1 tablespoon oil to the pan. Add the baby spinach and sauté until wilted, about 3 minutes. Add the garlic and sauté for 1 more minute. Remove the skillet from the heat.

5. Roll out the puff pastry onto the prepared baking sheet. Spread the onions over the pastry, leaving a 1-inch border. Top the onions with the mushrooms and spinach. Sprinkle the thyme over the filling and season all with salt and pepper.

continued

6. Fold one side of the pastry over to cover the filling and brush it with the egg. Fold the other side over. Use a fork to seal the pastry.

7. Turn the pastry over, seam-side down. Using a sharp knife, cut slits in a diamond pattern on the top of the pastry. Brush the pastry with the egg.

8. Bake for 20 to 30 minutes, until golden and flaky.

MAKE AHEAD: I prefer to make the filling 1 day ahead and store it in an airtight container in the refrigerator.

Per serving: Calories: 259; Total fat: 17g; Carbohydrates: 25g; Fiber: 3g; Protein: 4g; Sodium: 343mg

Cheesy Spaghetti Squash Noodle Bowls

Serves 4 / Prep time: 20 minutes / Cook time: 50 minutes

If cutting your spaghetti squash in half is difficult, microwave it on high for about 3 minutes to soften the flesh, which will make it easier to cut.

2 small spaghetti squash, halved and seeded

Salt and black pepper

½ (15-ounce) package frozen chopped spinach, thawed and drained

2 cups shredded mozzarella cheese, divided

¾ cup ricotta cheese

1 large egg, beaten

1 teaspoon Italian seasoning

¾ cup marinara sauce

1. Preheat the oven to 400°F. Line a rimmed baking sheet with parchment paper.

2. Coat the cut sides of the squash halves with cooking spray and season them with salt and pepper. Place them, cut-sides down, on the prepared baking sheet and roast for 35 minutes. Let the squash cool slightly.

3. In a large bowl, combine the spinach, 1 cup mozzarella, the ricotta, egg, and Italian seasoning. Season the mixture with salt and pepper.

4. Using a fork, scrape the strands from the squash, making sure to leave the shells intact. Add the squash strands to the ricotta mixture and stir to combine.

5. Place the squash shells, cut-sides up, on the same baking sheet. Spoon the squash mixture into the squash shells, top each with the marinara, and sprinkle the squash halves with the remaining 1 cup cheese.

6. Bake for 15 minutes. Let the noodle bowls cool for 10 minutes.

MAKE AHEAD: Store these baked noodle bowls, covered, in the refrigerator for up to 1 day.

Per serving: Calories: 416; Total fat: 24g; Carbohydrates: 30g; Fiber: 6g; Protein: 25g; Sodium: 824mg

Butternut Squash and Rice Casserole

Serves 6 / Prep time: 20 minutes / Cook time: 1 hour 15 minutes

Here is a casserole that works just as well for a weekend dinner as it does on your holiday table. It's very adaptable: Try adding steamed tempeh or sautéed spinach.

4 cups cubed butternut squash

2 tablespoons olive oil, divided

Salt and black pepper

1 red onion, chopped

1 tablespoon chopped fresh sage

2 teaspoons minced garlic

1 cup long-grain white rice

2 cups vegetable broth

2 large eggs, beaten

½ cup milk

1 cup shredded Gruyère cheese

1. Preheat the oven to 350°F. Line a rimmed baking sheet with parchment paper.

2. Spread out the squash cubes in a single layer on the prepared baking sheet, drizzle with 1 tablespoon olive oil, and season with salt and pepper. Roast for 15 minutes.

3. In a large saucepan, warm the remaining 1 tablespoon olive oil over medium heat. Add onion and sage and sauté for 8 minutes. Add the garlic and sauté for 30 seconds more. Add the rice and squash and sauté for 1 minute. Season with salt and pepper.

4. Add the broth and bring to a boil over high heat. Lower the heat to medium-low, cover, and simmer for 20 to 25 minutes, until tender. Remove the pan from the heat and stir. Cover and let rest for 10 minutes. Transfer mixture to a 9-inch square baking dish.

5. In a small bowl, whisk together the eggs and milk, pour over the mixture, and top with the cheese.

6. Bake for 30 minutes. Let cool slightly before serving.

MAKE AHEAD: Store this baked casserole, covered, in the refrigerator for up to 2 days.

Per serving: Calories: 331; Total fat: 13g; Carbohydrates: 43g; Fiber: 5g; Protein: 12g; Sodium: 299mg

Sheet Pan Mushroom Parmesan with Zoodles

Serves 6 / Prep time: 15 minutes / Cook time: 20 minutes

Any time I can enjoy all the flavors I love without a lot of effort, I am ecstatic. And I'm not the only one: This delicious one-pan recipe is always a crowd-pleaser.

3 medium zucchini, trimmed and spiralized

Salt and black pepper

6 large portobello mushroom caps

4 tablespoons olive oil, divided

1½ cups marinara sauce, divided

4 ounces fresh mozzarella cheese, shredded

¼ cup grated vegetarian Parmesan cheese

½ cup Italian bread crumbs

1. Preheat the oven to 375°F. Line a rimmed baking sheet with parchment paper.

2. Sprinkle the zucchini noodles with salt. Place them on paper towels and let them drain.

3. Brush the mushrooms with 2 tablespoons oil and season with salt and pepper. Place stemmed-sides up on the baking sheet and bake for 10 minutes.

4. Divide ½ cup marinara evenly among the mushroom caps. Top with the mozzarella and Parmesan.

5. In a bowl, toss the bread crumbs with the remaining 2 tablespoons olive oil. Sprinkle the mixture over the mushrooms and bake them for 5 minutes.

6. Add the zucchini to the baking sheet and bake for 5 minutes.

7. Blot the zucchini with paper towels, transfer to a bowl, and toss with the remaining 1 cup marinara. Top with mushrooms and serve.

SUBSTITUTE: Make this recipe gluten-free by using gluten-free bread crumbs. 4C makes a good variety that is easy to find.

Per serving: Calories: 259; Total fat: 16g; Carbohydrates: 21g; Fiber: 4g; Protein: 9g; Sodium: 460mg

Pad Thai

Serves 4 / Prep time: 20 minutes / Cook time: 11 minutes

If you love Asian flavors as much as I do, you'll definitely want to try this recipe. With crunchy vegetables in a creamy peanut sauce, it's both sweet and savory and you'll find yourself making it all the time.

8 ounces pad
Thai noodles

2 large eggs

Salt and black pepper

¼ cup peanut butter

1 tablespoon soy sauce

1 tablespoon freshly
squeezed lime juice

1 tablespoon grated
fresh ginger

2 teaspoons sugar

2 bell peppers, seeded
and sliced

1 cup shredded
purple cabbage

⅓ cup chopped peanuts

¼ cup chopped fresh
cilantro

1. Bring a large pot of salted water to a boil over high heat. Cook the noodles according to the package instructions. Scoop out and reserve ½ cup of the cooking water, then drain the noodles.

2. In a small bowl, beat the eggs and season them with salt and pepper.

3. Coat a large skillet with cooking spray and set it over medium heat. Add the eggs and cook until they are just set, about 3 minutes. Transfer the thin omelet to a plate and cut it into large pieces.

4. In a medium bowl, whisk together the reserved noodle cooking water and the peanut butter. Add the soy sauce, lime juice, ginger, and sugar and season the sauce with salt and pepper.

5. Transfer the noodles to a large bowl. Add the egg, bell peppers, and cabbage and toss with the sauce. Top with the peanuts and cilantro.

MAKE AHEAD: Store this pad Thai in an airtight container in the refrigerator for up to 3 days.

Per serving: Calories: 434; Total fat: 17g; Carbohydrates: 59g; Fiber: 5g; Protein: 14g; Sodium: 280mg

Loaded Potatoes

Serves 4 / Prep time: 20 minutes / Cook time: 1 hour

Smoky vegetables and black beans complement potatoes mashed with tangy Greek yogurt. Top them off with fresh cilantro and a squeeze of lime juice.

4 large russet potatoes, well scrubbed

1 tablespoon olive oil

1 onion, chopped

1 red bell pepper, seeded and chopped

2 cups baby spinach

1 large tomato, seeded and diced

1 teaspoon minced garlic

2 canned chipotle chiles in adobo sauce, finely chopped

1 (15-ounce) can black beans, drained and rinsed

Salt and black pepper

¼ cup plain Greek yogurt

½ cup shredded extra sharp cheddar cheese

1. Preheat the oven to 400°F. Line a rimmed baking sheet with parchment paper.

2. Pierce the potatoes all over with a fork, place them on the prepared baking sheet, and bake them for 50 minutes, or until tender.

3. Meanwhile, in a large skillet, warm the olive oil over medium heat. Add the onion and bell pepper and sauté for 6 minutes. Add the spinach and tomato and sauté until the spinach wilts, about 2 minutes. Add the garlic and chipotles and sauté for 1 minute. Add the black beans and sauté for 3 minutes. Season the mixture with salt and pepper.

4. Cut the potatoes in half and scoop out most of the flesh, leaving a ½-inch-thick shell. Put the flesh in a large bowl. Add the black bean mixture and Greek yogurt and stir to combine.

5. Place the potato shells on the same baking sheet. Spoon the bean mixture into the potato shells and sprinkle them with the cheese. Bake for 8 minutes, or until the cheese is melted.

MAKE AHEAD: Store these baked stuffed potatoes in an airtight container in the refrigerator for up to 5 days.

Per serving: Calories: 534; Total fat: 10g; Carbohydrates: 95g; Fiber: 15g; Protein: 21g; Sodium: 201mg

Spinach Calzones

Serves 4 / Prep time: 15 minutes / Cook time: 25 minutes

These crusty golden pockets are filling and taste sooo good. With creamy ricotta and melted mozzarella, they're always a hit with children and adults alike.

1 cup ricotta cheese

1½ cups shredded mozzarella cheese

¼ cup grated vegetarian Parmesan cheese

1 teaspoon minced garlic

½ teaspoon red pepper flakes

1 (15-ounce) package frozen chopped spinach, thawed and squeezed dry

Salt and black pepper

1 recipe Pizza Dough (page 178), unbaked

1 cup marinara sauce, warmed

1. Preheat the oven to 425°F. Line a rimmed baking sheet with parchment paper.

2. In a large bowl, mix together the ricotta, mozzarella, Parmesan, garlic, and red pepper flakes. Add the spinach and stir to combine. Season the mixture with salt and pepper.

3. Cut the dough into quarters and roll out each piece to a 7-inch circle. Divide the filling among the circles, placing it in their centers, and fold the circles in half to form half-moons. Press the edges of the dough with a fork to seal them.

4. Transfer the calzones to the prepared baking sheet and bake for 20 to 25 minutes, until golden brown.

5. When the calzones are nearly done, warm the marinara sauce in a small saucepan over medium-low heat.

6. Serve the calzones with the warm marinara for dipping.

MAKE AHEAD: Store these calzones in an airtight container in the refrigerator for up to 1 day or in the freezer for up to 1 month.

Per serving: Calories: 803; Total fat: 33g; Carbohydrates: 96g; Fiber: 7g; Protein: 34g; Sodium: 1392mg

More Creative Menus

THANKSGIVING GATHERING

Roasted Red Pepper Dip (page 26)

Kale and Roasted Beet Salad with Candied Walnuts (page 48)

Creamy Pumpkin Soup (page 68)

Cranberry-Apple Wild Rice Pilaf (page 123)

Festive Stuffed Squash (page 209)

Mushroom Wellington (page 215)

ROMANTIC DINNER

Fried Goat Cheese Salad (page 47)

Eggplant Moussaka (page 199)

PARTY BUFFET

Mediterranean Baked Feta (page 29)

Sun-Dried Tomato and Cream Cheese Stuffed Mushrooms (page 34)

Tomato-Basil Soup (page 59)

Fattoush Salad (page 52)

Greek Stuffed Peppers (page 213)

Produce Prep and Cooking Chart

VEGGIE / FRUIT	PREPPING OPTIONS	TOOLS
ACORN SQUASH	Slice off stem, halve, and remove seeds and pulp, then slice into wedges, puree, or dice	Chef's knife; spoon; food processor or blender
ASPARAGUS	Remove bottom third of the stalk, at least, to remove more fibrous ends; peel into ribbons lengthwise, slice into thin disks, or puree	Chef's knife; vegetable peeler; food processor or blender
AVOCADO	Slice in half lengthwise, twist to separate, and remove the pit using a knife; then slice into wedges or chunks, and slide a spoon between the flesh and skin to scoop out; puree or mash	Chef's knife; food proces mortar and pestle
BASIL, MINT, SAGE	Roll or stack to thinly slice; mash using a mortar and pestle or puree	Chef's knife; food proces mortar and pestle
BEETS	Slice off ends and peel, then chop or dice; spiralize red beets; puree, peel into ribbons, or grate	Chef's knife; paring knife vegetable peeler; spiraliz food processor or blend box grater
BELL PEPPERS	Place a pepper on a workspace with the stem facing up and slice the side "lobes" and the bottom off, then discard the seeds, pith, and top (which should be all connected as one piece); slice into lengths, dice, or puree	Chef's knife; food proces or blender

/ COOKED	COOKING METHODS	SERVING IDEAS
ed	Roast; sauté; steam; braise; slow cook; pressure cook	Stuffed roasted halves; roasted wedges; soup
cooked	Roast; steam; sauté; simmer; slow cook; pressure cook	Salad; add to pasta, legume, grain, and vegetable dishes; soup; pickled; risotto; anything with eggs, such as quiche
cooked	Grill; fry	Add to salads, sandwiches, and pasta; guacamole; place wedges on toast and top with olive oil, salt, and pepper; anything with cooked eggs, such as omelets; add to smoothie; use in a sauce or dressing
cooked	Sauté; roast; simmer	Pesto; add to salads, vegetables, grains, legumes, pasta, and eggs; add to dressings and sauces; add to pizza and breads, such as foccacia
cooked	Sauté; roast; simmer; steam; bake; slow cook; pressure cook	Chilled soup with sour cream and dill; pickled; add to salads, pasta, grain, and vegetable dishes; add puree to breads and chocolate cake batter; ravioli filling or pasta dough; add spiralized noodles to soups or use as pasta noodles; bake as chips; raw slaws; sauté with butter and maple syrup
cooked	Roast; sauté; simmer; bake; grill; stir-fry; slow cook; pressure cook	Roast and peel, slice in half, seed, and drizzle with olive oil, plus capers, garlic, salt, and pepper; puree as soup; add to tomato sauces; stuff whole with grains and vegetables; add to salads, sandwiches, grains, legumes, and pasta; raw with a dip; add to bread; add to a soffritto of onion, celery, and carrots; add to sauces such as aioli

VEGGIE / FRUIT	PREPPING OPTIONS	TOOLS
BOK CHOY	Slice off root end and use whole or chop	Chef's knife
BROCCOLI	Trim fibrous ends and snap off leaves, peel off the outer tough skin, and separate florets by slicing through the stems; slice the stems into batons, thinly slice into disks, chop, or dice	Chef's knife; food proce or blender
BRUSSELS SPROUTS	Trim bottoms and remove any wilted or yellowed leaves, thinly slice, halve, or grate	Chef's knife; food processor fitted with a grater; mandoline
BUTTERNUT SQUASH	Slice off ends, cut the squash in two just above the bulbous end, stand on end, and peel with a sharp knife or vegetable peeler; scoop out seeds with a spoon; slice into wedges, chop, dice, puree, or spiralize	Chef's knife; food proce blender; spiralizer
CABBAGE	Slice into wedges, thinly slice, or grate	Chef's knife; box grater
CARROT	Trim top, and peel; slice, dice, grate, or peel into ribbons	Chef's knife; paring knif box grater; vegetable p
CAULIFLOWER	Trim bottom and remove leaves; slice into steaks; cut off florets at the stems; chop or dice stems; grate into rice, puree, or mash	Chef's knife; paring knif box grater; food proces or blender

W / COOKED	COOKING METHODS	SERVING IDEAS
/ cooked	Braise; grill; sauté; simmer; roast; stir-fry; steam	Warm or raw salad; raw slaws; soup; ramen; add to grain, vegetable, and legume dishes; raw with a dip for an appetizer; pickled; add to a green smoothie
/ cooked	Bake; blanch; braise; fry; grill; roast; sauté; simmer; steam; stir-fry; slow cook; pressure cook	Add to egg dishes, such as casseroles and quiche; roast with olive oil, smoked paprika, salt, and pepper, and finish with lemon juice; stir-fry with other vegetables in sesame oil, and finish with soy sauce; add to raw salads, Buddha bowls, grains, legumes, and vegetable casseroles; roast and toss with pasta, capers, preserved lemon, grated Parmesan cheese, and toasted bread crumbs; soup; add roasted broccoli to pizza toppings
/ cooked	Roast; bake; steam; braise; fry; sauté; grill; pressure cook; slow cook	Slice thinly for a raw salad with green onions and dried cranberries; roast with apples; make a hash with potatoes, onion, and apple cider vinegar; toss with garlic, spices, and olive oil and throw on the grill; bake into a cheesy gratin
ked	Roast; sauté; steam; simmer; slow cook; pressure cook	Stuff with grains and/or vegetables; spiralize into pasta; add to salads, grains, legumes, and vegetables; soup; risotto
/ cooked	Roast; braise; sauté; steam; grill; bake; stir-fry; slow cook	Roast wedges rubbed with olive oil, garlic paste, salt, and pepper; braise red cabbage with olive oil, apple cider vinegar, brown sugar, and apple chunks; slaw; cabbage rolls stuffed with rice and vegetables; pickle for kimchi; topping for tacos
/ cooked	Roast; braise; sauté; steam; grill; bake; stir-fry; slow cook; pressure cook; simmer; steam	Raw in a salad; soup; slaw; soufflé; bread; cake; add to vegetable, grain, and legume dishes; simmer in a pan with butter, honey, and orange juice until all the liquid is gone except a glaze
/ cooked	Bake; blanch; braise; fry; grill; roast; sauté; simmer; steam; stir-fry; pressure cook; slow cook	Puree into a sauce; grate into rice for tabbouleh or risotto; roast whole, smothered with a spicy sauce; substitute it for chicken in many dishes; soup; pickle for kimchi; swap out potatoes in mashed potatoes; use in a gratin; toss with pasta, lemon, capers, and bread crumbs

VEGGIE / FRUIT	PREPPING OPTIONS	TOOLS
CORN	Remove kernels by standing a cob up in a bowl lined with a towel. Anchor it with one hand, and slide a knife down the cob to slice off the kernels.	Chef's knife
CUCUMBER	Peel, halve, and scrape out juicy seeds; slice into thin or thick slices, peel into long ribbons, dice, grate, or pickle	Vegetable peeler; chef's knife; paring knife; spoon; box grater
DELICATA SQUASH	Slice off the ends, halve, and scrape out the seeds; slice into half-moons or puree	Chef's knife; spoon; food processor or blender
EGGPLANT	Slice off the ends, cut into ¾-inch slices, sprinkle evenly with salt, lay in a colander to drain for 30 minutes, then rinse to remove the salt and pat dry; slice, chop, dice, mash, or puree	Chef's knife; colander
GARLIC	Peel. Chop the bulbs, thinly slice, mince, or smash and lightly salt to form a paste	Chef's knife
GINGER	Peel with a spoon and trim; slice, mince, or grate	Spoon; paring knife; fine grater or zester
GREEN BEANS	Trim; slice lengthwise or slice crosswise on the diagonal	Paring knife; chef's knife

/ COOKED	COOKING METHODS	SERVING IDEAS
√ cooked	Sauté; roast; simmer; steam; grill	Chowder; stew; add to tacos with black beans, tomatoes, and avocado with a squeeze of lime; sauté with pickled onion, basil, and tomatoes and stuff into peppers with a little cheese; risotto; toss with zoodles, mint, and tomatoes; make Mexican corn
√ cooked	Sauté; bake; stir-fry;	Use in salads, especially Greek and Middle Eastern salads; make tzatziki; swap out bread for cucumber disks; pickled; chilled soup; make a sandwich with cream cheese and dill; add slices to jugs of water; sauté with a little butter, salt, pepper, scallions, and mint
ed	Roast; bake; sauté; simmer; grill; braise; steam; slow cook; pressure cook; stir-fry	Soup; stuff scooped-out half with grains, dried fruits, and other vegetables; drizzle with oil and garlic, sprinkle with salt, pepper, and cayenne, and roast; add to warm salads or Buddha bowls; use as a pizza topping; toss with pasta; add to tacos; puree to add to chilis and stews; bake into a gratin
ed	Bake; roast; sauté; simmer; grill; stir-fry; braise; slow cook; pressure cook	Mash into a dip such as baba ghanoush; marinate and grill for a sandwich with tomatoes and smoked mozzarella; lightly bread and bake in a tomato sauce topped with Parmesan; roast and stuff with a grains and pomegrante seed salad; simmer with tomatoes, onion, garlic, and balsamic vinegar and puree for a soup
√ cooked	Roast; sauté; blanch; bake; stir-fry	Wrap a head of garlic with a drizzle of olive oil and a sprig of rosemary in foil and roast; sauté or roast chopped or thinly sliced garlic with vegetables, legumes, or grains; add to a soup with onions and thyme
√ cooked	Simmer; sauté; stir-fry	Tea; add to broths and soups; grate finely to add to fruit with a squeeze of fresh lime; add to miso and garlic paste to rub on vegetables; gingerbread; add to sauces or jams
ed	Blanch; sauté; simmer; bake; roast; stir-fry	Add to salads, soups, and grains; roast with olive oil, thyme, salt, pepper, and a squeeze of lemon

VEGGIE / FRUIT	PREPPING OPTIONS	TOOLS
JALAPEÑO PEPPERS, SERRANO CHILES	Trim off the stem, slice in half, and remove the seeds and pith; slice, dice, or mince	Paring knife
KALE	Fold leaves over the central tough rib, and remove the rib with a knife (not necessary for baby kale); coarsely chop	Chef's knife
LEEKS	Cut and discard the top part of the leek with tough, dark green leaves, split in half lengthwise, and feather under cold running water to remove dirt; slice into thin half-moons	Chef's knife
MANGO	Slice "cheeks" of mango off from stem to end, parallel and as close as possible to the long, flat pit; score the cheeks down to, but not through, the skin using the tip of a sharp knife; turn the cheek 90 degrees and score again. Scoop out the mango chunks using a spoon; puree.	Paring knife; food proce or blender
MUSHROOMS, SMALL	Wipe clean with a paper towel and slice, quarter, or mince	Chef's knife
OLIVES (GREEN, NIÇOISE, KALAMATA)	Slice, smash using the flat side of a chef's knife, coarsely chop, or leave whole	Chef's knife
ONION, SHALLOT	Chop, dice, grate, or slice	Chef's knife
PARSLEY, CILANTRO	Position a sharp knife at a 45-degree angle to the herbs and slice across the leaves to coarsely chop, including stems; gather the leaves and stems together and chop into smaller pieces or continue chopping to mince	Chef's knife

W / COOKED	COOKING METHODS	SERVING IDEAS
/ cooked	Sauté; roast; bake; stir-fry	Roast with corn bread batter; roast with cheese; add to vegetable and legume dishes; pickle; add to cheese sandwiches or quesadillas; use in traditional tomato salsas or ones with diced pineapple and mango; jelly
/ cooked	Sauté; blanch; bake; roast; stir-fry; simmer; braise; grill; steam	Pesto; baked kale chips; sauté with lemon, olives, and capers, and toss with quinoa; add to soup; braise with garlic, dried chipotle chiles, and tomatoes; add to a green smoothie
/ cooked	Sauté; roast	Raw in salads; add to sautéed or roasted vegetables; roast halves in the oven with olive oil, salt, and pepper
	Bake; grill	Smoothie; soup; sauces; relish with bell peppers, black beans, jalapeño, and shallots with a squeeze of lime juice; add to salads; add the puree to pound cake, muffins, pudding, ice cream, or sorbet; dry into fruit leather; spring rolls
/ cooked	Sauté; bake; stir-fry; roast; braise; grill	Coat with olive oil and a dusting of salt and pepper and roast at 400°F until well-browned; add to pasta and grain dishes; make mushroom risotto; stuff with peppers, garlic, bread crumbs, and Parmesan cheese for an appetizer; use in casseroles
/ cooked	Sauté; roast	Add to pastas, grains, vegetables, and legumes
/ cooked	Bake; braise; fry; grill; roast; sauté; stir-fry; pressure cook; slow cook	Stuff sweet onions with grains and other vegetables and roast; caramelize and add to sandwiches, burgers, grains, and legumes; make a flatbread with caramelized onions, ricotta cheese, and herbs
/ cooked	Suitable for all kinds of cooking	Add to most vegetable, pasta, grain, and legume dishes, including roasts, soups, and casseroles

VEGGIE / FRUIT	PREPPING OPTIONS	TOOLS
PEAS	Pry the shells open with your nails or a small knife, and remove the peas; puree or leave whole	Food processor or blender
PORTOBELLO MUSHROOMS	Wipe clean with a paper towel and scrape out the gills using a spoon; leave whole or slice	Chef's knife; spoon
POTATOES, WHITE, RED, YUKON, FINGERLING	Peel (or not), slice, dice, mash, puree, grate, spiralize, or smash	Vegetable peeler; chef's knife; paring knife; potato ricer or masher; box grater; spiralizer; food processor (using pulse only); mandoline
RADISHES	Trim roots and tops; leave whole, halve, or thinly slice	Paring knife
SCALLIONS	Trim roots and remove any outer damaged sheath; leave whole, slice in half lengthwise, or chop	Paring knife; chef's knife
SPAGHETTI SQUASH	Cut in half or leave whole; scoop out seeds and pulp with a spoon; after cooking, run the tines of a fork across the flesh to pull up "spaghetti" strands	Chef's knife; spoon; fork
SPINACH	Stack leaves, remove stems (not necessary for baby spinach), roll into a fat cigar shape, and thinly slice; gather slices together and mince	Chef's knife
SUGAR SNAP PEAS, SNOW PEAS	Trim ends and leave whole or thinly slice	Paring knife; chef's knife

/ COOKED	COOKING METHODS	SERVING IDEAS
cooked	Bake; blanch; braise; sauté; simmer; steam; stir-fry	Add to pasta, casseroles, soup, and vegetable dishes; puree for a pea soup; lightly sauté with salt and pepper, and toss with mint; add to an asparagus quiche or omelet
cooked	Grill; roast; sauté; braise; bake	Use in place of a bun for veggie burgers; stuff with vegetables, grains, or legumes; marinate in olive oil, balsamic vinegar, and garlic and roast or grill
ed	Bake; braise; fry; grill; pressure cook; roast; sauté; simmer; slow cook; steam; stir-fry	Twice-baked potatoes whipped with soft cheese topped with chives; spiralize and toss with olive oil, salt, and pepper, and roast until browned; grill slices of potato to add to salads; potato gratin; smash roasted baby red potatoes, sprinkle with salt, pepper, and dried rosemary, and drizzle with olive oil; roast; hash browns
cooked	Bake; braise; fry; stir-fry	Bake or roast with butter, salt, pepper, and parsley; add to salads
cooked	Braise; roast; grill; sauté; stir-fry	Toss in olive oil, salt, and pepper and roast or grill; pickle; add to salads, soups, pasta, grains, pizza, or legume dishes; add to any kind of egg dishes
ed	Roast; bake; pressure cook; slow cook	Stuff with black beans, roasted red peppers, and onions, and top with cheese; toss strands with olive oil, Parmesan cheese, salt, pepper, and roasted pumpkin seeds
cooked	Blanch; braise; sauté; simmer; stir-fry	Sauté in a little olive oil, salt, and pepper, and toss with cooked quinoa, yellow raisins, and a squeeze of lemon; add to soups, salads, sandwiches, and pasta; mince for spanakopita
cooked	Bake; braise; grill; roast; sauté; steam; stir-fry	Toss in olive oil, salt, and pepper and grill, then toss with chopped mint before serving; sauté and sprinkle with sea salt; sauté in sesame oil, and finish with lemon, salt, pepper, and sesame seeds

VEGGIE / FRUIT	PREPPING OPTIONS	TOOLS
SWEET POTATOES	Peel with a vegetable peeler; slice, dice, chop, grate, spiralize, or puree	Chef's knife; vegetable peeler; spiralizer; food processor or blender; box grater
SWISS CHARD, MUSTARD GREENS, DANDELION GREENS	Remove the central fibrous stem, if applicable, and stack several leaves on top of one another; fold in half lengthwise, roll into a fat cigar shape, and slice crosswise into wide or narrow ribbons; gather ribbons together and finely chop or mince	Chef's knife
TOMATOES	To peel a tomato, score the skin on the bottom of the tomato with an X, blanch in simmering water for 20 seconds, then dip in a bowl of ice water, and peel starting at the X; slice, chop, dice, grate, or puree	Paring knife or chef's kni box grater; food proces or blender
ZUCCHINI, SUMMER SQUASH	Trim the ends and chop, dice, or slice into rounds, wedges, or matchstick lengths; grate using the largest holes of a box grater; spiralize	Paring knife or chef's kni box grater; spiralizer; fc processor or blender; mandoline

W / COOKED	COOKING METHODS	SERVING IDEAS
oked	Roast; bake; sauté; simmer; grill; steam; slow cook; pressure cook	Baked and stuffed; spiralized; puree for a sauce, soup, or to add to pancake batter; add to stews and chili; enchiladas; tacos; season, roast, and add to warm salads and Buddha bowls; add to root vegetable roasts and gratins; baked sweet potato chips; sauté with butter and maple syrup; season and bake sweet potato fries; hash
/ cooked	Bake; blanch; braise; roast; sauté; simmer; steam	Use Swiss chard leaves for rolling up grains and vegetables, cover with a pasta sauce and cheese, and bake; sauté Swiss chard stems separately with garlic, salt, and pepper, finished with a vinegar drizzle; sauté garlic and onion, add broth, salt, and pepper, and braise mustard greens until tender; sauté dandelion greens in olive oil, garlic, salt, pepper, and red pepper flakes
/ cooked	Bake; blanch; braise; fry; grill; roast; sauté; simmer; stir-fry	Stuff raw with chickpea or lentil salad; slice in half and slow-roast with garlic, salt, and pepper; panzanella bread salad; tomato jam; salsa; Caprese; bruschetta; gazpacho
/ cooked	Bake; grill; roast; sauté; simmer; steam; stir-fry	Bake as fries: slice into wedges, toss in olive oil, salt, pepper, oregano, and Parmesan cheese; spiralize for spaghetti, then toss with tomatoes, basil, and garlic; slice in half lengthwise, then slightly hollow out to make boats and stuff with vegetables and grains topped with pasta sauce and cheese

Measurement Conversions

VOLUME EQUIVALENTS	U.S. STANDARD	U.S. STANDARD (OUNCES)	METRIC (APPROXIMATE)
LIQUID	2 tablespoons	1 fl. oz.	30 mL
	¼ cup	2 fl. oz.	60 mL
	½ cup	4 fl. oz.	120 mL
	1 cup	8 fl. oz.	240 mL
	1½ cups	12 fl. oz.	355 mL
	2 cups or 1 pint	16 fl. oz.	475 mL
	4 cups or 1 quart	32 fl. oz.	1 L
	1 gallon	128 fl. oz.	4 L
DRY	⅛ teaspoon	—	0.5 mL
	¼ teaspoon	—	1 mL
	½ teaspoon	—	2 mL
	¾ teaspoon	—	4 mL
	1 teaspoon	—	5 mL
	1 tablespoon	—	15 mL
	¼ cup	—	59 mL
	⅓ cup	—	79 mL
	½ cup	—	118 mL
	⅔ cup	—	156 mL
	¾ cup	—	177 mL
	1 cup	—	235 mL
	2 cups or 1 pint	—	475 mL
	3 cups	—	700 mL
	4 cups or 1 quart	—	1 L
	½ gallon	—	2 L
	1 gallon	—	4 L

OVEN TEMPERATURES

FAHRENHEIT	CELSIUS (APPROXIMATE)
250°F	120°C
300°F	150°C
325°F	165°C
350°F	180°C
375°F	190°C
400°F	200°C
425°F	220°C
450°F	230°C

WEIGHT EQUIVALENTS

U.S. STANDARD	METRIC (APPROXIMATE)
½ ounce	15 g
1 ounce	30 g
2 ounces	60 g
4 ounces	115 g
8 ounces	225 g
12 ounces	340 g
16 ounces or 1 pound	455 g

Index

About the Author

Wendy Polisi is the passionate cook, photographer, and blogger behind WendyPolisi.com. When she is not in the kitchen, chances are you will find her at a theme park with her kids. She lives in Orlando, Florida, with her husband and three children.